On the Big Rivers

On the Big Rivers

FROM THREE FORKS, MONTANA TO NEW ORLEANS, LOUISIANA

Richard E. Messer
with Jerry D. Sanders

Published simultaneously in Canada, the United Kingdom, and the United States of America by Genoa House. For information on obtaining permission for use of material from this work, submit a written request to:

permissions@genoahouse.com

Genoa House
www.genoahouse.com
+1-905-906-7799

Many thanks to all who have directly or indirectly provided permission to quote their works. Every effort has been made to trace all copyright holders; however, if any have been overlooked, the author will be pleased to make the necessary arrangements at the first opportunity.

Book design by iWigWam
www.iwigwam.com

Front cover image *After the Rain—Fort Peck Lake* © is from an original painting by Carole Kauber.

DEDICATION

To the rivers of North America and those who love them.

"I do not know much about gods; but I think that the river
Is a strong brown god—sullen, untamed and intractable . . .
The river is within us, the sea is all about us."
The Four Quartets, The Dry Salvages
—T.S. Eliot

"You must give
to the river
the kindness
you would give
to any brother."
—Chief Seattle

ACKNOWLEDGMENTS

I wish to express my thanks to Carole Kauber for her loving support and to Marylyn Rands for her brilliant and tireless proofreading. Thanks to Patty Cabanas, whose faith in this manuscript inspired me and who was always there to help me along. I'd also like to thank my daughter, Anne Slatton, for her careful reading and editorial suggestions. Dick Sugg, Eddie Williams, and Norm Rehm, my river buddies, all helped with this writing in different ways and I thank them. A special expression of gratitude and a powerful thank you to Jerry D. Sanders. Without him this trip would not have taken place, nor could I have written this book without his help and inspiration.

FOREWORD

Jerry (Deacon) Sanders not only conceived this trip down the Missouri and Mississippi rivers in 1962, he planned it, outfitted it, and paddled it with me 3,800 miles from Three Forks, Montana to New Orleans, Louisiana.[1] When it came to writing this narrative, he supplied aid and advice throughout, as well as writing some of it, in that I quote from his river journals extensively. So while this is my recounting of our voyage, limited mainly to my experience of it, he has in many ways co-authored it. Friends we have been since college, river buddies and friends for over fifty years, and friends we will be, as far as breath can carry us.

What follows is a story of a friendship forged through trials and triumphs. It is also the tale of a wilderness initiation, of how I came to know the sort of man I am and the sort of country I live in. Most of all it is the story of our adventures for three and a half months in 1962 on the two rivers that form the fourth longest river system in the world. Writing this narrative of our journey and thus reliving it over fifty years later, I was struck by the singularity of our experiences. Such a journey, in this day of the internet, is no longer possible. Also, both rivers have changed drastically, especially the upper Missouri, where we were on a river that had transformed since even so recently as the voyage that James Schultz recounts in his *Floating on the Missouri,* written in 1902. It is a nostalgic voyage for Schultz in that he means to visit places on the river he knew twenty years before as a young man in what was still aptly

---

1   Jerry D. Sanders. Letter to author, April, 2014. Jerry writes: "Inspiration for taking the Queen to New Orleans? When I was 12-13 years old, I saw a movie of floating the Bighorn River through its canyon. The floaters ran rapids, caught big trout. But the showstopper, the image tattooed in my mind, was their discovery of two skeletons, one of a man and one of a grizzly bear. Near the skeletons were the rusted remains of a muzzle-loading rifle. So a man was out adventuring and met his fate. The floaters who found this were having an adventure which included burying the skeletons, taking the grizzle's skull and the rifle for booty, or more practically, as proof. This all set my mind to having an adventure of my own."

called the Wild West. Only once does he mention Lewis and Clark, rather disparagingly, but it is clear that their Voyage of Discovery, made a hundred years before his, was on a river that was much more pristine than the one he traveled. And now, over two hundred years after Lewis and Clark, the river they knew no longer exists and, in fact, has been replaced in many areas with despoliation beyond their imagining. This is a great loss for our country and the only saving grace at this writing is that many conservation groups now focus on working to protect the rivers and that more and more people are becoming aware of the issues involved.[2]

I had planned to write this book soon after the voyage. Life, as they say, pushed aside my plans and it is only now that I have finally come around to setting down our experiences. In this accounting of our trip, written so many years later, what emerges is not only the tale of our adventures, but a historical document. It is, for me, a personal history that reflects the growth of my understanding and values. It is also historical in the sense that Jerry and I were pioneers of a river journey that has been done by many others since 1962. Further, it seems to me that America's rivers, and particularly the Missouri and the Mississippi, are wonderful repositories of the history of our country. In writing about our encounters along the rivers, on the water and in the towns, I found that time and again those experiences embodied the energies and archetypal images that have fueled our national development, beginning with the earliest European voyages to our shores to the present day.

The lure of the American Eden, land of economic opportunity, of freedom from tyranny, from oppression in any form, home of rugged individualism and unlimited personal growth, the headlong optimism of westward expansion and the Doctrine of Manifest Destiny—all these "ideas" and their consequences, good and bad, were dramatically played out over the years along the banks of America's two greatest rivers. From

---

2 A great example of such folk is Janet Moreland. Her source to sea: Brower Springs, MT to the Gulf of Mexico, solo kayaking expedition on the Missouri and Mississippi in 2013, is a marvelous contribution in this area. Her love of the rivers and of sharing her adventures on them goes hand in hand with her mission, which includes, as she says, ". . . elements of education, environmental stewardship, and empowering youth, women, and men to confidently pursue their dreams." Quoted from her website, http://loveyourbigmuddy.com.

among these images, the one that stands out for me and to which I speak most directly is that of the struggle for human rights.

Still, my primary task is to stay faithful to the feelings and perceptions of the young man I was at the time. The facts of the journey are valid in that I have trusted to Deacon's journal as well as my own, accounts written on the spot, for what happened when and how each of us felt about it. I have tried to avoid self-serving embellishments, but occasionally I comment on the story from my present perspective, and I'm sure at times my nostalgia for those days colors my narrative. Regarding this, I trust or at least hope, even the most exacting of readers, those who have run the rivers themselves, will indulge me.

CONTENTS

I

A DREAM OF ADVENTURE

In the spring of 1962 I was living in Boulder, Colorado and had just finished my first semester in graduate school; I had no job and I was scheduled to tie the knot with my fiancée, Gloria Welsch, in the fall. What to do? Should I dig in, find some sort of work, prepare for another semester in grad school? Or take off with my Wyoming buddy, Jerry Deacon Sanders to paddle a canoe from Three Forks, Montana to New Orleans, 3,800 miles down the Missouri and Mississippi rivers? To say my choice to go with Jerry was a no-brainer would be accurate in more ways than one.

Gloria and I talked over the proposed trip. I presented it as a kind of extended bachelor's party, jokingly. In kind, she asked if I were sure she would be demurely waiting when I returned, if I returned? That question hung in the air between us for a moment. She was an art major; I wanted to be a writer. Neither of us were the most stable people in the world and this was the sixties. All I could say, really, was that, yes, I *hoped* she would be. And no worries, she wouldn't be lucky enough to get out of the engagement that easily. Jerry and I, or at least Jerry, had everything planned out to the last detail, including the coming back part.

In my own mind, I felt there would be plenty of time to buckle down and get into some kind of career harness once we were married. I knew she would be busy all summer, finishing up her last semester before graduating. And if I did find work, any job I got would be part-time and low paid. This might be my last chance to go on a real adventure. I had to go.

Over the next few weeks we didn't talk about it much; tacitly we just both accepted it was something that was going to happen. It was an exciting time. I was teeming with eagerness to test my mettle, and I imagined the river as a kind of final frontier, not fully explored, still to a large degree unknown and mysterious.

The "awakening" of the sixties has become a cliché by now. The spirit of that decade, lively and enthusiastic in the beginning, optimistic about change, became dark and troubled. But I had just read Jack Kerouac's *On the Road,* and I shared his vision of America as the land of spiritual opportunity. I was determined to experience life on the open road as he had. However, my journey would be from West to East and North to South, and my road would be the fabled river system of the Big Muddy and the Mighty Mississippi. Then there was simply the epic scale of the trip. No one, as far as we could determine, had ever done the entire 3,800-mile trip in a canoe with no motor, in a single summer. If we did get to New Orleans by the end of September, we would have done something to be proud of.

Of course, neither of us wanted to think about the journey in such grand terms. Certainly, when Jerry first asked me to go with him, I just thought of it as the chance for an adventure. In fact, though I had been along when he bought the used eighteen-foot aluminum Grumman canoe in Denver, it was a mutual friend of ours, Al, who was supposed to ride shotgun as bow paddler, not me. That changed on a chill April morn when the three of us ventured out on a pond to learn something about how the craft handled. Al leaned too far right. As we dragged the half drowned canoe and ourselves up the muddy embankment, he announced that all bets were off; he had better things to do with his summer, or at least safer, drier things. I don't recall exactly how making the decision went for me from there, but I know I decided right away that the Deacon, as we call him, was not doing this trip by his lonesome.

No one else stepped up, so, by way of what may have been a process of elimination, I became part of the planning for this epic voyage, slated to be the number one bow paddler.

Looking back, I know the prospect of going on such a trip should have intimidated me, at least a little. True, growing up in Colorado on the Western Slope, born there, I had plenty of experience camping and climbing. I was of the mountains and in the summers spent time trekking all through them, especially Lookout Mountain, whose foothills began in my backyard. However, I also grew up in poverty. Therefore, though I was a fisherman from my bent-pin days on, and owned a twenty-two rifle, a Remington bolt-action repeater, I didn't have the wherewithal to be a hunter. My granduncle, Jimmy Wyatt, a World War I veteran, had a 30.06 rifle that my dad inherited when Jim died and I cleaned that rifle several times, but that was as close as I came to going out after deer or elk with it. In truth, I was not brought up in the cowboy traditions of the West; my people were from Kentucky on my father's side and Illinois on my mother's. I was tall, gangly, shy and given to reading books and daydreaming. The fact that my father had ridden the rails in the thirties during the Great Depression, knew the hobo jungles in Indio, California and other places, that he liked to go down from our house to where the bums slept on cardboard pallets by the tracks and talk to them and trade stories and had even written some good poems about his times on the road, made a deep impression on me. It lifted my imagination into the realms of romantic adventures and somehow the seal was set upon my heart to become a writer.

As I say, I knew my share about wilderness camping, hunting, and dealing with nature first hand. I had trapped muskrat and sold the pelts in high school through every fall and winter. Each summer of my adolescence I had spent many hours in the Colorado River, going down with my brother Steve and our friends to a sandbar near home, swimming across, or tubing through the bucking waves down to where the Roaring Fork River flowed into it. But I hadn't been in a canoe before the spring of '62. I knew little more about paddling than which end was supposed to go in the water. Still, I figured I could read all about J strokes and pitch strokes in one of Rutstrum's books. Once I got on the river, I was sure it would all come naturally.

Figure 1.1 Betty and Jerry, Gloria and Rich[3]

Headwaters of the Missouri River

On June 3, 1962, six of us, Jerry and Betty, his girl at the time, Gloria and I, and two friends of Jerry's, Nik, and Jim, got into Jerry's green '54 Ford and drove to Three Forks, Montana, headwaters of the Missouri River. The canoe, which Jerry, always one for the irreverent pun, had christened, *The Afrigin Queen,* was strapped to the top of the car and we were all in high spirits. These days, Three Forks advertises itself on its internet site as a town that figures very importantly in the famed journey of Lewis and Clark: *"Heralded in history, basking in natural splendor . . . [that] can look back to its past with awe . . ."* True enough, but in those days what we saw as we drove in was a small, quiet Western town, largely uncelebrated and just beginning to build up its tourist trade. We found a friendly café on Main Street and sat at a big round table made of heavily varnished knotty pine. There was a lot of laughter and kidding.

3 All photos in this book are courtesy of Jerry D. Sanders, 1962, unless otherwise noted.

By the time the second pitcher of beer started around, Nik was shaking his head, saying we would last no more than a month on the water but that should be long enough to cure our insanity. It took several hours to finish that meal. It was getting pretty drunk out by the time we piled back into the car and drove outside town to camp by the river.

As the sun rose the next morning, all of us were up and into the car despite our varying degrees of hangover. We drove back to the same café and sat at the same big round table. But we weren't as boisterous as we had been the day before. We said little and focused on our food. The fact that Jerry and I were actually going to do this thing had begun to sink in. Neither of the women was happy about it. I remember Gloria, after having kept pretty quiet all morning, smiled wryly at me and nodded toward my plate of scrambled eggs.

"You better dig in," she said, "It'll be a while before you get another decent meal."

There was both concern and jeering in her voice. I didn't have a witty reply handy.

An hour later we were on the riverbank nervously going over again the list that Jerry had compiled of towns along the river where we would stop for mail. Glo and I shared a kiss and hug. She promised to write; I promised to write and to take care, and by 9:30, goodbyes said all round, grub box and gear loaded, we were ready to go.

Shoving off onto the back of that powerful, brimful river felt good. Jerry in the stern of the canoe shouted a farewell and I turned to wave at the four figures dwindling back there on the bank. Then we were around a bend and on our way.

Someone in the group took a photo that I still have of Deacon and me, heading off that June morning, paddling the 18-foot *Queen* out into the roiling waters of the Missouri, bound for New Orleans. In the photo we look high of heart and ready for anything. We look, untried greenhorns that we were, like we actually know what we're doing.

Figure 1.2 Bound for New Orleans

Those first few hours we fairly flew along without much effort, glancing back occasionally at the snow-capped Bitterroot Mountains where Lewis and Clark had once crossed westward to the Colombia River. Waterfowl, mostly geese and ducks started up occasionally in front of us. The river was high and fast, carrying snowmelt from a long winter and runoff from recent rains. As we paddled, the sky gradually paled to gray, but the rain held off. By noon the current had begun to slow. The river widened until it seemed like we were on a lake. This made no sense until we rounded a bend and came upon Toston Dam. This was our first dam and it wasn't supposed to be there.

Toston Dam at that time had no generators and therefore produced no electricity. It was primarily for irrigation. Only a few hundred yards across, it didn't stand very high, perhaps sixty feet. Either it wasn't big enough or was too recently erected to even be noted on the 1:500,000 maps we had. Since it wasn't marked, we weren't ready for it.

With no idea of how we would portage around, we paddled toward what looked like the best place to go ashore. Near the dam, not too far from where we pulled in, a man was squatting, fishing pole in hand. We went over to talk to him and it turned out his father was the caretaker for the dam. He pointed to a gravel road above the riverbank that we hadn't been able to see from the water, a service road. He wished us good luck on our voyage and after we had reconnoitered a bit we found the road provided an easy portage route, though we had to make two trips.

Soon we were on our way, energized by having accomplished our first portage and feeling ready to tackle any challenge the river might offer. As if in reply the wind came up. It began blowing upstream into our faces with such force that it seemed we were paddling up river, not down. We pushed on, determined not to let a little wind dampen our spirits.

This was my first taste of "the wind factor." Jerry had some previous experience with canoes and other watercraft. This was my first time canoeing a river. I was doing some on the job training as far as handling a paddle, and more than that I was learning how to paddle in tandem with someone. As bow paddler, I set the pace and Jerry synchronized his stroke with mine. It took some concentration and a long series of adjustments, but gradually we seemed, for the most part, to have settled into a strong, steady rhythm. Still, after three hours, rhythm or no, I was ready to quit. But we kept paddling. Both of us were determined to put in a full day before heading in to set up camp. We knew we would never make it to New Orleans, not before winter anyway, if we didn't, right off the bat, get used to paddling at least eight to ten hours a day. The hours wore on and my arms wore out; they felt leaden and numb, my back and shoulders ached. And we kept paddling.

Finally, as the long afternoon waned, the wind eased off. I looked up from my paddling trance at the sound of splashing and saw half a dozen geese just ahead herding broods of grayish yellow goslings along the near bank. Travelling more or less silently we often surprised deer, mostly mule deer, and waterfowl, many ducks, blue herons, and later, pelicans, mergansers, cormorants, and other wild life that otherwise we might not have seen. Gazing after the geese, I saw that the sun was low over the hills. The river was in deep shadow. Around us, steep rocky slopes rose almost directly from the water and flattened out into a gently rising plateau that ran to the distant mountains on both sides. An hour or so earlier, we had gone past an area of beautiful and bizarre rock formations where layers of rock were heaved nearly perpendicular. To the southwest, far off, I could see snowy peaks, but from where we were down on the river I couldn't get any real sense of the mountain range. Still, I felt the immense and rugged presence of the mountains out there.

We paddled on. Gradually, ranch buildings and power lines, even roads and vehicular traffic became more and more scarce. Civilization was falling away behind us. I didn't have to say anything or turn around to glance at Jerry to know we were both sharing this thought. Nonetheless, far scattered though they might be, there were occasionally houses. In fact, our campsite for that first night, a small cove between two rocky outcroppings, turned out to have a house directly across from it, high up above the riverbank. I saw it as we disembarked and thought of telling Jerry we had to push on, but my fatigue got the better of my love of wilderness.

A few minutes later we were bustling around on shore, one of us unloading the tent gear, the other setting up what we needed to cook our dinner and gathering driftwood for a fire. Our sleeping quarters were to be basic, not to say crude. Jerry had picked up the tent, along with several other items, from an army surplus store. It was a vintage military pup tent of the sort that hadn't changed much since the Civil War, constructed out of two sections of heavy olive drab canvas called shelter halves that had to be attached to each other by a row of metal buttons. The tent had no floor, stood three feet at its peak, and had just about enough space inside for two old fashioned blow-up air mattresses with sleeping bags laid out on top. This outfit, poles and all, weighed about ten pounds. The two sections had to be unbuttoned every morning and attached every night, but they were waterproof (almost) and perfect for wrapping up our other gear into neat bundles.

One good thing about canoe travel, especially in an eighteen footer, is that you can carry a lot of gear along, much more than you would be comfortable with packing on your back. On the other hand, there was the business of portaging to consider. Today we had had to empty the canoe, carry all our gear a hundred yards, then go back, heave the canoe onto our shoulders and tote it around a dam to the river and reload it. Since there were fifteen dams in all to portage, it was important to make sure that we had only essential equipment along. Grub box, tent, ground cloth, sleeping bags, cooking gear, clothing, first aid kit, toilet paper, two towels, hand axe, 6-volt flashlight, maps: these were all crucial. We each had personal toiletry items. For me that meant a contact lens case and fluid, though soon I was wearing the lenses continuously 24/7. Mosquito dope and hats were a must, but we had forgotten about sunscreen. Both our noses were sunburned after that first day and we quickly learned to make "nose-shields," covering them with folded pieces of thin cardboard fitted under our sunglasses. In addition, thinking that we might have to live off the land at some point, or at least supplement our food supply at times, Jerry tucked his rifle and a box of shells into the tent roll. This little Remington single shot model 4 rolling block .22 was handy, good looking, small, light, and yet accurate within its range—a good gun for our needs. I threw in fishing gear: hooks, bobber, a trotline, but no pole or reel. I wanted to be low key about the fishing bit, since I definitely wasn't prepared to buy a license in each of the states we passed through. A camera, a book or two and our journals, those items were necessities also. Our cooking gear we kept simple: two mess kits, a skillet, and a wire grill to cook on over the open fire, dish cloths, soap, and a mesh copper pan scrubber called a Chore Girl. At the last minute I had decided to throw in my cast iron Dutch oven. Many times that summer I would curse myself for bringing along such a heavy and cumbersome item, but it always served well enough. We had tea, two tins of Dinty Moore stew, biscuits and syrup. Easy to make and, tired as we were, absolutely delicious.

It rained lightly as we prepared dinner, but not enough to put us off. By the time we finished eating it had stopped and we sat down near the tent for a smoke—not cigarettes, they were too expensive, even then, and too hard to keep dry in the wet and rain. We had brought pipes and now sat smoking Union Leader, looking out over the glassy, sunset-reflecting water. We had put in a decent day's paddle, portaged our first dam, and we felt pretty satisfied with ourselves. We had something like 2,400 miles to go before we hit the Mississippi, then only 1,300 or so to New Orleans.

Figure 1.3 Camp on Lake Sewell, June 5

The next morning I got up just as the sun began to climb over the bluff above the river and fill our little cove with light. It was a beautiful morning with no clouds in the sky and the river flowing past smooth and serene. I made a fire and started boiling water for tea and rice. Jerry rolled out and began jingling the gear together. We loaded the canoe, arranging things a little more efficiently than we had the previous day. Both of us were a little stiff and sore from yesterday's workout, but by the time we had finished our breakfast we were eager to take on another day's paddling—even though by then it had started raining. As often happens in the mountains, what had started out as clear fine weather, changed completely in an hour's time. We started off in a downpour, which stayed with us on and off most of the day. I was soon wet, despite my poncho.

Around noon we took a break on shore to build a fire and dry out. We ate some of the provisions we had bought in Three Forks, made and drank bouillon, and set off again, feeling pretty good. The rain had stopped or at least paused. With each mile we paddled, we were getting deeper into what I thought of as "the real country," steep banks, rocky outcropping, pine ridges running back from the water, and no signs of human habitation. On the other hand, the current gradually became negligible, the river widened, and very soon it was replaced by a seemingly endless expanse of slack water.

Initiation

We had come into our first lake, a reservoir really, created by the river piling up against Canyon Ferry Dam. The transition between river and lake had an eeriness about it. As we paddled, it was as though I could feel the river slow and shudder and finally die. Bobbing logs, huge tree branches, and debris of all kinds multiplied and became hazardous. Raucous magpies flew back and forth ahead of us and stands of silvery, skeletal trees began to appear, some only half drowned, others, farther out, showing just their topmost branches. There were goose or blue heron nests among the leafless limbs, but no birds. For a time it was like we were paddling along in a littered Sargasso Sea or watery graveyard. Then, as we passed the last of the dead trees, the wind, having a good clear shot at us across the miles of flat water came up fast at near gale force. It didn't take much wind out on the lake to build waves high enough to capsize us if we hit them wrong. Still tired from yesterday's long push, I was quick to agree with Deacon when he suggested we quit fighting it and make camp.

Having eaten and feeling refreshed, I walked with him up through the cedars nearby to explore the area a little. Jerry has a note in his journal that he shot a cottontail, but whether we cooked it up or not, neither of us remembers. I do recall fishing, with no happy result, and setting a trotline.

The wind blew hard that night. I woke several times to the ominous sound of the tent flapping as though it were about to become airborne, and I prayed the gale would play itself out by morning.

Sure enough the next day dawned clear and calm. But my relief was short-lived. An hour or so after we had eaten, loaded up, and left the cove, the wind found us again. It got bad and the spray from waves slapping the bow soon had me wet and cold. Once again we decided to go ashore and built a fire to dry out a little. We made tea, ate a couple of peanut butter and jelly sandwiches, then set out again, doggedly determined to get far enough down the lake that we could camp and make the dam the next day.

Later, I learned that actually there were two Canyon Ferry dams: one built in 1889 with a modest lake behind it, Lake Sewell. This first dam was dismantled and the present, much larger dam, completed to replace it in 1954, created Canyon Ferry Lake, which eventually swallowed Lake Sewell, the town of Canton, and over four thousand acres of farmland to boot, becoming the third largest body of water in Montana, twenty five miles long and, in places, five miles wide.

Soon we got a vivid sense of the immensity of this lake. By noon it was so wide we weren't sure where we were or how far it was to Canyon Ferry Dam. Paddling along the shore was out of the question because the bays were so large. Trying to navigate down the center of the waterway was not an option either, not if we wanted to minimize the distance from point A to point B and thereby save time and paddle strokes. To ensure that we were keeping to the shortest possible route, Jerry had to keep track of where we were on his map.

I'm not talking about a *Rand-McNally* here. At his feet he had a cardboard tube full of rolled geological survey maps of the Missouri River put out by the Corps of Engineers, both the upper Missouri and the lower. Occasionally, as now, he would call out for me to hold up and I would look over my shoulder and see him with one of the maps spread across his knees, puffing on his pipe, staring down at the mapped course of the meandering river to see how we could save time by cutting across from one bend to another in as straight a line as possible.

This is what he was doing when I asked him about the clouds over in the southwest.

"Yeah," he said. "I've been watching 'em too."

In fact, we had both seen them grow from specks to puffballs as we paddled.

"You think it's a storm?" I asked, knowing full well he would say something like: Does the bear shit in the woods?

Which he did, then added that if we could make a cut across the lake at this point, we'd be only an hour or so from the dam and in great position to tackle the portage tomorrow morning. We might hit some wind, but he thought we could make the crossing before the storm arrived. I agreed. We were co-captains in most ways, friends and equals, partners—but the idea for the voyage was his, as was the canoe and more than half the equipment. These facts generally meant that I, unconsciously for the most part and often automatically, went along with his opinions and druthers on most important decisions. This would create some problems later on, but for now the issue came down to one thought for me: dangerous or not, we would save several miles of paddling.

So we gave it a shot.

The clouds on the horizon above the far mountains were still puffs, but now they had darkened. The crossing was at the most three miles. Three miles of open water against the wind—toward those clouds. We would be in trouble if a storm did blow in. On the other hand, the clouds looked so far away. They might miss us entirely. And I could see, tiny in the distance, a boat cruising around a distant point.

After an hour of hard paddling the wind stiffened. This was a bad sign. We had reached the middle of the crossing, there was no turning back, and it had become only too damned obvious that a storm was heading our way. We were going to have to really dig in to make shore before it hit. The water grew choppy, then much rougher, and soon we were bucking through three-foot waves and paddling like hell. At first it was a challenge, it was fun, and I felt my strength as I shoved the paddle blade out there, caught water, and pried it back. But the far shore came no closer. As we crested a wave, I saw the boat, or thought I did, still cruising, perhaps watching us from across the lake. I dug in hard, but we were virtually paddling in place, tread-milling.

The wind now turned vicious, ripping at us full blast. Then with incredible swiftness the storm was on us. There was no sky, only massive low clouds and horizontal rain and whipping wind. The waves, driven from the distant shore, pushed and rolled under and all around us. They mounted quickly to four and five feet high. I realized we were paddling into a vast bay, headed for its center. The piney shore looked as if it were receding into the small end of a telescope.

Jerry yelled a string of obscenities and we both pitched into our paddling in deadly earnest. For the first time I felt fear rising in my stomach. A wave broke over the bow and gunwales into my lap, followed by another and another. The thin plastic Salvation Army poncho I wore was next to useless. I didn't like getting completely soaked, but the thought of the stores getting wet and the canoe shipping enough water to founder us sent my mind racing over what little I had read about dealing with such a situation. Jerry from his position in the stern was doing all he could to keep us tracking bow forward into the waves. I knew we had to meet them as straight on as we could and not get sideways to them or the wind. I focused on catching each wave with my paddle at the right moment and angle. That helped a little. But I couldn't tell if we were making the rocky shore come nearer.

When I looked up again, the shoreline seemed tantalizingly close, maybe a half mile away. That half mile was the hardest, a real killer. Neither of us had any strength left; we were paddling on sheer adrenaline, terrified that our trip was over before it had really begun. We were digging in, trying to heave the canoe ahead across the waves from crest to crest and more often than not the next wave was breaking over our bow and we were dipping into the next trough and splashing through the next crest. We were shipping lots of water so that the *Queen* began to wallow, floundering.

"Paddle!" we shouted to each other.

And we did. We paddled hard and fast and kept paddling; the pines and rocks of the shore loomed a little closer. I could see the cove we were heading for, a narrow strip of beach along the wide bay. My back, between my shoulder blades, hurt, and my throat was raw. My lungs were on fire and my heart was pounding harder than it ever had. To quit paddling was not an option. Time and again waves went crashing over us. Yet, slowly, stroke by agonizing stroke, we were making headway. And after an interminable time, we entered the relatively calm water of the cove.

Stumbling out of the canoe, into the driftwood cluttered shallows, both of us grabbed the bow rope, pulling the *Queen* ashore over the sand and rocks with the last of our strength. I sank to the ground and lay flat on my back, totally winded, wondering if I were having a heart attack. Jerry stood gazing around a moment, exercising his Captain's responsibility of checking things out.

"Hey," he gasped, "this is a damn picnic area."

Then he collapsed beside me.

Gradually, I got my breath back. After a time the pain in my chest eased, and I looked over to see how Jerry was. He was up, moving gingerly around what was sure enough some sort of a public area with several tables and a few standard issue metal cook-boxes, grills and all. Not too far off, newly constructed cabins were spread evenly up the slope. We were close to a real estate development of some kind, probably vacation homes. Somehow, that made what we had just gone through feel even worse.

"You ok?" Jerry asked, staring at me.

"Maybe we should call it a day," I said, trying to laugh. I was thinking that for all our effort we had made a grand total of about six miles.

"You ain't wrong on that one, partner," he said. "Verily and amen."

We laughed, but the river had almost had the last laugh.

We were just beginning to understand why the Missouri is called, *Ol' Misery*. Too true. Our third day out had come close to being our last.

Oh, yes, we had life jackets and we'd put them on. But later in the voyage we were told of several boys from a Boy Scout camp on Fort Peck Reservoir who had drowned just the day before our arrival. They were caught out in a storm in their canoes and capsized—drowned with their life vests buckled on. When the waves get high and wild enough, you drown from what is called, "mouth immersion." If the water gets to really slapping you around, it's hard to keep from ingesting some and it doesn't take much to go from coughing to drowning. This is a fact I am just as glad we didn't know at the time.

I woke early the next morning and lay awake in the pre-dawn grayness awhile, thinking about how close we had come to real disaster. I thought of Gloria, I thought of what little family I had. A feeling of something like remorse passed over me. I didn't want to die like some smart aleck greenhorn far from home. Definitely, I had overestimated my abilities and underestimated the river. This discouraging thought, for whatever reason, made me even more determined to complete the voyage.

Portaging Canyon Ferry, Hauser, and Holter

There are fifteen dams on the Missouri river. Ten are in Montana. One, Garrison, is in North Dakota, and the others, Oahe, Big Bend, and Fort Randall, are in South Dakota, with the last dam, Gavins Point, straddling the border of South Dakota and Nebraska. Toston, small and easy to get around, had lulled us into thinking that this portaging of dams, hassle that it was, ultimately wasn't so bad.

So, the day after the storm, humbled, but still confident in our ignorance, we prepared for our first major portage with little trepidation. Our routine, pretty much established by now, was to paddle till near sunset, make camp, and get up late the following morning, past eight, have a leisurely breakfast and light out for a vigorous paddle till one or two, then break for lunch. On this morning, while Jerry snoozed, I rousted myself early, just to get out of the tent. It was not really a place where you wanted to lay awake, imagining disasters.

I stood for a moment, gazing around at the half completed housing development and up at a low, gray sky. Everything was wet—soaked. Previous campers had left firewood though, and I was able to jingle up enough fairly dry kindling to make a fire. I had set a trotline the night before, but the storm had washed in a lot of driftwood and now as I stood looking at the debris littered shoreline, I almost decided to forget the line, just abandon it as I had the last one. Instead, I set about untangling it and luckily my efforts were rewarded with a beautiful rainbow trout.

Fried up and added to our usual portions of rice, it made a great breakfast.

We paddled at a pretty good pace, despite sore muscles from losing yesterday's race with the storm. Our plan was to do the portage before dark. But, lo! Just around the first big bend we came upon a concrete wall over two hundred feet high and a thousand across: Canyon Ferry Dam.

Again we found a road, a highway actually, running along beside the river. After tying off the canoe, we struggled up the ninety-foot talus embankment and walked down the pavement to the dam. A thorough reconnoiter revealed no easy way to portage. We decided the only thing to do was to make two trips of about a mile each, down the highway to the dam, across the top of the dam, then along the road on the other side to a place where we could rope the canoe, partially loaded with gear, gingerly down the bank to the river again.

Figure 1.4 Tailwater of Canyon Ferry Dam

It was a long, challenging portage. Hoisting the emptied canoe by rope up the ninety-foot loose shale slope to the highway and carrying it along the highway and across to the access point went well enough. The *Queen* is a light girl, about 75 pounds. But toting the grub box, tent and bedding, paddles, and life preserver cushions and more up the loose shale, across the dam, and down to the river was hard work. For the first time I realized the cast iron Dutch oven, though it may have fit nicely in the Conestoga wagons of yore, had no place in our canoe. It took several hours before we lugged everything across and down to the water, reloaded the *Queen*, and set off.

It was exciting to be heading down a "free," swift river again. Even though the current slowed a mile or so below the dam, I could still feel it lending its power to my every stroke.

"You know what I think?" Jerry sang out behind me.

"That we should get rid of the Dutch oven?"

"No, no," he laughed. "Just thinking about the grub box."

"You're hungry? We can't stop this early."

"No, man. I just had this eureka moment. We tie the grub box to the gunnels, right?"

I had to turn half around now and check out the expression on his face.

"Okay," he said, grinning at me. "Bad idea."

How could it be a bad idea to secure our food and gear? I was about to argue when I realized he was, indeed, dead right.

"Oh, man," he continued. "Yeah, if we had gone over yesterday in that storm? Hell, the weight of the gear and grub box would have overcome the canoe's flotation and dragged it to the bottom, leaving us very much up a creek, my friend, in wild waves with nothing but our paddles."

We hooted about this, incredulous at our stupidity and luck. This was just one of many things we had failed to anticipate. With us it was always—learn hard, but learn.

We camped in a glen about six miles below Canyon Ferry Dam. Dusk came on as we sat by the fire. The sky was free of ambient light and as night came on it filled with a billion stars. The Milky Way star river sparkled brilliantly. I fell asleep, reminding myself not to forget this time: the smoky smell of the green pine bough burning low and the sound the river made going its way on and on.

The next morning, Friday, June 8, having slept well and taken our time with eating, we got back on the water about nine. This day was to be our first full day of blessed sunshine—which meant, all ye water gods be praised, smooth water and very little wind!

Usually on the upper Missouri below any of the dams, the river drops back into its natural channel, more or less, and flows along at a pretty good pace. We were now riding a swift, free flowing current. It was easy paddling through this beautiful mountain country. But not for long. Happy as I was with the warmth and clear skies of the day, I was disappointed to see the river widening and the current going slack again. After not even an hour, we were coming into the lake behind the next dam: Hauser.

Figure 1.5 Gates to the Mountains

At present, Hauser Lake is only fourteen miles long and was probably less back in '62. I was thankful that though this lake was wide, it was not nearly as wide as Canyon Ferry. With the wind gone we paddled along peacefully, close to the shoreline, following or being led by a heron. He would flap off from somewhere along the bank, land, and then as we neared, he'd flap up again. The time went quickly on the smooth, broad water. By noon we made the dam.

To our relief it was only half the height of Canyon Ferry. After a relatively easy portage, we were over it and back onto the river again. Again the current was alive and powerful; we encouraged it by paddling hard, enjoying the speed and the sense that we were making up for lost time—really getting somewhere. Here we had our first stretch of rapids, mild and not long enough, but after all those hours on the lake with the wind in our faces, this first taste of white water was truly exciting.

Soon we were in a canyon with walls made of massive, rugged outcroppings of rock, running right up from the river for at least a thousand feet.

"This is great country, isn't it?" Jerry said. "Man, look at that over there!"

I turned to see him point out a big bald eagle in a tree by the river, its white head and tail feathers clearly visible.

"This is what they call Gates to the Mountains," he added.

He had shown me this section of the river on the map earlier. As I gazed at the great gray rock shelves rearing virtually straight up out of the water on both sides, they did look like giant gates and they seemed to open as we paddled toward them, only to be replaced by yet another pair of gates just beyond. Lewis and Clark had marveled at these formations and the beauty of the area. Lewis wrote,

> . . . this evening we entered much the most remarkable clifts that we have yet seen. these clifts rise from the waters edge on either side perpendicularly to the height of 1,200 feet. every object here wears a dark and gloomy aspect. the tow[er]ing and projecting rocks in many places seem ready to tumble on us. (spelling and punctuation are Lewis')[4]

A somewhat less well-known comment follows.

---

[4] Fred Bergson, ed. *The Journals of Lewis and Clark,* (New York: Penguin Books, 2003), 196.

Jerry's Journal, Friday, June 8

. . . crazy cliffs, perpendicular, thrust fault gray lime stone, towering out of river. Saw an otter swimming along cliff face just above waterline, carried its young up into another cave. In the water, head poked up, it looked like a sea serpent, silver brown on neck, body a deep silky brown. Ferocious, it made a sound between a grunt and a growl.

Later, having made camp, we went up Elkhorn Creek, also called Willow Creek, to fish. Caught none. Saw the Jellystone beaver, completely unafraid. Stared at us; we poked at it. Finally it moved on.[5]

The Gate to the Mountains is one of the most beautiful spots we hit on the upper Missouri. The river here seems bottomless. Looking out over the dark green water flowing smoothly between the cliffs, I felt its massive power, yet all was peaceful and serene. For the first time, though oft repeated, I wished I had done more reading in the last few months about the river, the history of sites we were passing, and the geology of the country. I was tempted to argue for setting up camp for a week or so on one of the piney beaches between the cliffs, but, of course, we couldn't spare the time. All the way down the river we couldn't afford to stop anywhere long enough to really explore and enjoy a particular landscape or town. We always felt we had to push on.

On this day, having made a good camp at Elkhorn Creek, we tried to catch a few fish. I could actually see trout, probably brookies, in the clear ripples along a stretch of sandy bottom, or lurking in the eddies behind boulders, but they weren't interested in anything either of us had to offer. So, instead of fried trout, we devoured one of our staple dinners, Kraft mac and cheese. Then we enjoyed an evening smoke in the absence of all noise except the breeze and the lapping of the water.

The next morning we left the stunning, beautiful scenery of the "Gates" area and paddled on to Holter Dam, a distance of twenty miles.

---

5   Jerry D. Sanders. Unpublished journal. All journal entries in this book, unless noted as the author's, are courtesy of Jerry D. Sanders from 1962 river trip. Entries dated, but without pagination.

Holter was our fourth dam so we felt pretty cocky as we approached it. And, sure enough, we got the canoe and gear across the dam and down to the river again in less than an hour.

Below Holter, we hit Wolf Creek Canyon and rode some rapids at a brisk pace. The white water might have been classified as two, verging on three. Later on we were to encounter some class four rapids—serious white water. But, in any case, at the time we knew nothing of the classification system for rapids, other than fun and exciting, oh-oh, dangerous, and, holy crap, suicidal!

We passed Tower Rock, which had not been "developed" yet as a camping area. It was grayish rock and not very tower-like, unless you were talking about a crumbling tower. Still it was majestic. We had lunch nearby and I enjoyed stretching my legs a little along the bank. Setting out again early in the afternoon, we decided we might as well paddle on a few more hours and try and make the town of Cascade. We pushed hard and there was plenty of light left when we paddled into shore just below the town, tied up, and walked in.

Cascade, Montana

This was our first stop for a mail check and cleanup. We had looked for a post office at Canyon Ferry, but there was none. Walking into Cascade after less than a week on the water, it felt strange to encounter sidewalks, buildings, cars, and to wait for traffic until a light turned green. People tended to stare at us, even in this early phase of the trip. We ignored them or grinned back and went on to the Post Office and the General Delivery window.

Later, in the dim, smoky interior of the Sportsman Club, we bellied up to the bar. A cold beer had never tasted so good. I was into a strong buzz with the first few swallows. Now everything looked fresh and interesting and the world seemed a mighty fine and friendly place. I went to the Men's shortly, and, of course, it was a typical lavatory, none too sanitary, its walls etched with graffiti. But it had hot running water and a urinal—and a flush toilet. I couldn't help reflecting that our species, given what I'd been experiencing lately, had made some pretty significant progress over the eons, at least materially. When I returned to take up my seat beside Jerry, he was talking genially with two men along the bar. This sort of thing happened a lot during our voyage. Jerry, of middle height, dark haired, with an open, friendly expression and always looking to make a new acquaintance or discover something of interest wherever he was, never shied away from talking about the river trip, or anything, really, that intrigued him. And, as his nickname implied, he could tell a tale as well as any of the raconteurs of old. Deacon had a wonderful eye for detail and mimicry and humor came naturally to him. Telling stories, listening to the other fellow's stories, trading lies, as he said—this was and is his stock in trade. He was an English Major in college and from childhood on an outdoorsman and hunter with a love of nature's beauty. His good-natured extroversion helped both of us out of more than one fix along the way, not to mention that it earned us a few free beers to boot.

Before long, deep in conversation though we both were with the two men, it became clear that if we were going to have dinner and be sober enough to eat it, let alone get back to camp, we had better push away from the bar. The bar and the restaurant were interchangeable so all we had to do was step over to one of the tables by the far wall. The menu was chalked up on a large blackboard nearby and it took only a few words to the barkeep to order. Soon, he was setting down before us two platters laden with hamburgers slathered in onions, a crisp dill pickle slice and a side of fries. I still remember how happy I was not to be digging into another batch of mac and cheese.

It was dark by the time we left the Sportsman. We weren't about to scout around for an ideal camp site, which meant that we ended up sleeping where we had come ashore—next to a dump. I woke just after dawn, head aching, and gazed out at a big concrete sewer pipe and tangles of litter. Where was I? Who was I? Turning to look the other way, I saw a wheat field. Then I remembered—I was canoeing the Missouri River, heading for New Orleans; it was Saturday. Unimpressed, I closed my eyes and it was near midmorning before I woke again. I roused Jerry, we ate, and finally, got back on the water.

On cue, it began to rain.

I put on my poncho automatically, as did Jerry. We had learned to keep them handy. The current had slowed and that made paddling in my poncho even drearier. Adding to my despondency was the realization that we had left the Rockies behind, passed out of the awe-inspiring mountains, and entered the semi-arid high plains country of Montana. Since the landscape was flatter, the river was slower and more meandering—we were travelling huge oxbow loops now. Still, the riverbanks were green with willows, sumac, tall grasses and a few trees, which made them a natural gathering place for birds and many geese. Up on the plateaus on either side of the river, the spring grass was knee high. We saw a couple of white tail deer just after setting out, and in the distance, a small band of antelope.

I noticed that the river, clear and green two days ago, had now begun to change to the muddy brown color it is known for. The transformation from green to brown wouldn't be complete until after we came into Great Falls. There, at the confluence of the Sun River, which drains the agricultural lands of the plains and picks up a lot of soil, the Missouri is two colors for a time. After Great Falls the muddiness of the Sun River wins out. Even here below Cascade, however, I could see why Mark Twain supposedly said, "The Missouri River is too thick to drink, and too thin to plow."

Continuing to paddle north, northeast, as though we were heading to Canada, we navigated the long loops up to Ulm, had lunch near it, and went on. Jerry shot a goose from the canoe with his little .22 rifle. We were in what looked like unpopulated, open country, but still I was a little leery about the shots being heard. Poaching is something highly frowned upon by the Sheriffs of Nottingham wherever you roam. Yet, so far we had seen no sign of Game and Fish personnel. I was hoping it would stay that way.

We weren't far from Great Falls by now. We paddled until late in the evening, hoping to at least make the outskirts. The miles crept by. I tried to focus on catching glimpses of wildlife, but I was thinking about the number of dams that awaited us in Great Falls, wondering how we would manage those portages. My chest was aching by the time we decided to call it a day, far short of our destination.

By luck, we found a good campsite as the sun was about to set. The latest of the rain showers had begun to slack off, and by the time we had bustled around, putting the tent up and building the fire, the sky had cleared.

Whenever the rain stopped our moods improved; our optimism returned. Surely, tomorrow the sun would be out all day and the wind would be at our backs. Meanwhile, we cooked up Mr. Goose and he was delicious!

Jerry's Journal, Monday, June 11

Made Cascade last night, dropped down completely out of the mountains to the High Plains. Eight to ten inch grasses, green everywhere. Ate dinner in Cascade at the Sportsman's Club—drank a six-pack—kind of light headed. Left the next morning late and made it past Ulm where we ate lunch. I killed two magpies. Rain, rain, rain. Finally let up in the afternoon late. River is no longer the clean river of the mountains. It is wide silt filled brown yellow flow of whirlpools, sucker billows and changing currents; brush and trees and weeds clutter the edges. But the grass filled plains rise above.

Shot a Canadian honker that afternoon, fried it for dinner—built the fire on the riverbank, tent on hill above. Shot a Great Horned Owl in flight—nice shot. Saw first jackrabbit just outside Cascade. Saw white tails and a herd of antelope. Haven't caught any fish yet.

Great Falls area has fabulous homes on heights, slums on riverbank. No really prominent skyline, some radio towers and a couple of tall buildings. Jets always flying over. Can barely see the mountains we came out of—the Big Belts.

You might think from this that Deacon was up and firing at everything that moved. Not so—and even less so as we paddled farther north and east. But he was, after all, a hunter, born and raised, and part of our plan had been to live off the land if we could. I guess the counterpoint to his entry is a sentence or two of mine for Monday, June 11. I wrote, "At the laundromat in Great Falls. There is a good-looking blonde here who has been nice to us despite our shaggy appearance." This is followed immediately by, "Sent cards to Gloria and to my grandmother." I'm sure Gloria, back in summer school, studying hard, writing me long, loving letters, would not have enjoyed that bit of juxtaposing. Frankly, I don't remember the scene too well and Jerry's journal entry doesn't mention it at all. Evidently, no more than occasional glances were exchanged with the blonde. I do know that I was sorely missing Gloria and a sentence later all I have to say is: "Soon our clothes will be ready and we will go on to attack the dams—three in five miles, then camp for the night."

II

DAMN DAMS

The map on Figure 2.1 depicts the dams we encountered at Great Falls. Our portages and campsites are also marked. It is to be especially noted that here at Great Falls the river drops over 600 feet in ten miles. There once were five waterfalls in this stretch, the highest of which was named The Great Falls. It was originally 87 feet high. These falls were seen as an ideal site for hydroelectric dams and over the years five have been built here: Black Eagle, Rainbow, Cochrane, Ryan, and Morony. As a result of this construction all the falls but one, Crooked Falls, have been defaced and submerged.

Back in 1805, it must have been a spectacular sight that Lewis and Clark came upon as they reached the waterfalls that June. Though it took them a month to get around them (now that is a portage), Meriwether Lewis wrote that they were a true American wonder, sublime, the grandest sight he'd beheld thus far in the journey of the Corps of Discovery.

I can't resist setting down the famous excerpt from his diary, describing the party's first coming on what was even then called, The Great Falls of the Missouri.

> . . . my ears were saluted with the agreeable sound of a fall of water and advancing a little further I saw the spray arrise above the plain like a collumn of smoke which would frequently dispear again in an instant caused I presume by the wind which blew pretty hard from the S. W. I did not however loose my direction to this point which soon began to make a roaring too tremendious to be mistaken for any cause short of the great falls . . . I hurryed down the hill which was about 200 feet high and difficult of access, to gaze on this sublimely

grand specticle . . . immediately at the cascade the river is about 300 yds. wide; about ninety or a hundred yards of this next the Lard. Bluff is a smoth even sheet of water falling over a precipice of at least eighty feet, the remaining part of about 200 yards on my right formes the grandest sight I ever beheld, the hight of the fall is the same of the other but the irregular and somewhat projecting rocks below receives the water in its passage down and brakes it into a perfect white foam which assumes a thousand forms in a moment sometimes flying up in jets of sparkling foam to the hight of fifteen or twenty feet and are scarcely formed before large roling bodies of the same beaten and foaming water is thrown over and conceals them. In short the rocks seem to be most happily fixed to present a sheet of the whitest beaten froath for 200 yards in length and about 80 feet perpendicular, the water after descending strikes against the butment before mentioned or that on which I stand and seems to reverberate and being met by the more impetuous courant they role and swell into half formed billows of great hight which rise and again disappear in an instant. This butment of rock defends a handsom little bottom of about three acres which is deversified and agreeably shaded with some cottonwood trees; in the lower extremity of the bottom there is a very thick grove of the same kind of trees which are small, in this wood there are several Indian lodges formed of sticks . . . from the reflection of the sun on the spray or mist which rises from these falls there is a beatifull rainbow produced which adds not a little to the beauty of this majestically grand senery. After wrighting this imperfect discription I again viewed the falls and was so much disgusted with the imperfect idea which it conveyed of the scene that I determined to draw my pen across it and begin agin. . . but then reflected that I could not perhaps succeed better than pening the first impressions of the mind . . . l hope still to give to the world some faint idea of an object which at this moment fills me with such pleasure and astonishment . . . (spelling and punctuation are Lewis')[6]

---

6   Fred Bergson, ed. *The Journals of Lewis and Clark,* (New York: Penguin Books, 2003), 160-1.

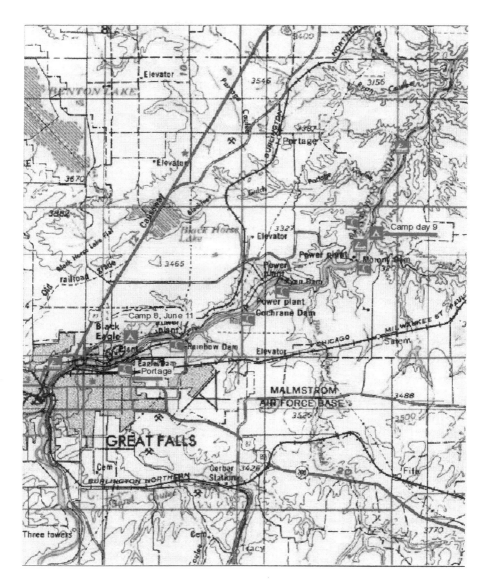

Figure 2.1 Map of the river at Great Falls[7]

I envy Lewis this magnificent, pristine view. I mourn the fact that it has long since been blotted out and no longer exists for the appreciation and enrichment of all. Time and again on our journey, Jerry and I noted

7 All four maps in this book are courtesy of www.mytopo.com.

how the inroads of civilization had scarred the once beautiful landscape. And as I write this narrative the situation has only gotten worse. I know that every Eden has to be destroyed; that is the way of our species. If we want the wonders electricity can provide, even at the basic level of warmth and shelter, we generally have to sacrifice the wonders of natural beauty. Still, it is a terrible loss and our human legacy is impoverished a bit more each time and in whatever form it happens.

Even before we portaged Black Eagle, as Jerry noted in his journal quoted above, the blight that follows our civilization's version of progress was all too obvious. Since we were down on the river, we weren't seeing the more dressed up parts of the city that the Chamber of Commerce might have pointed to proudly. Looking across at the brushy banks, we saw junk everywhere, construction refuse, cast off appliances, tires, and even rusted hulks of cars. As Jerry pointed out, up on the high hills above the river there sat large, fabulous homes. Down on the bottoms you saw trailers and shacks, slums. The magnificent roar of the falls Lewis had heard was now replaced by the din of traffic and if you looked up you saw billboards and a crisscross of white jet trails.

Remembering how I felt at that time, I can't continue without being pulled back to Lewis' diary entry cited above. Did you notice his tucked away reference to the native folk of this Eden?

> ". . . the butment of rock defends a handsom little bottom of about three acres which is deversified and agreeably shaded with some cottonwood trees; in the lower extremity of the bottom there is a very thick grove of the same kind of trees which are small, in this wood there are several Indian lodges formed of sticks . . . from the reflection of the sun on the spray or mist which arrises from these falls there is a beatifull rainbow . . ."[8]

He notes the "stick" lodges without comment; he has commented often enough before on what he considers the primitive conditions and behaviors of the Native Americans that the party encounters. He and Clark both address them in their formal speeches as: "Children."

---

8 Fred Bergson, ed. *The Journals of Lewis and Clark,* (New York: Penguin Books, 2003), 160-1.

Or sometimes," Noble Children." Referring to them in his journal, he often calls them, "Savages." Generally, his tone is objective, as one might expect in a "scientific" report that he knows will come under the scrutiny of President Jefferson and ultimately the public at large. Nonetheless, he had no doubt he was a member of a culture and race superior in everyway to these native peoples. He felt that neither he nor his culture had anything of true importance to learn from them. His mission as an explorer was informed by the tenets of Manifest Destiny, which these days seems to include all the universe, known and unknown.

But I digress; my intention really is to have us pause a moment and think of those people in those few lodges on the island. Lewis looked down on them from above, literally and figuratively. He kept them physically and psychologically at a distance. The Indians, like the whites, were no angels, of course. Still, on the whole they had been hospitable to the white trappers and traders they encountered. They weren't above stealing horses; some tribal groups like the Sioux could be hostile and violent, but most historical accounts show that up until the end of the eighteenth-century the native populations of this country were more sinned against than sinning.

Certainly they did not deserve the fate lying in wait for them. Australia publicly apologized for its near genocide of its indigenous populations in 2008. But many other countries, including the U.S. and Canada have yet to formally express any sense of moral responsibility for their genocidal ways. Robert Manne puts it well in his recent article on the Australian apology.

> First, settler societies find it peculiarly difficult to apologize to those peoples whose conquest and pacification is the condition of their existence. Those who settled in what became the United States of America have found it easier to offer apology to those they transported as slave labor from Africa than they have to the Native Americans that they dispossessed.

The Guardian, 5/26/2013.[9]

---

9 http://www.theguardian.com/profile/robert-manne.

So it goes. Certainly at age 23, though I had had more than a few experiences with Native Americans, I'm sorry to say I felt no moral pangs regarding their past or present treatment. Even when farther down the Missouri, an Indian man stopped for me and gave me a ride into town in the back of his pickup with his friends, my sole reflection at the time as I shared a beer with them was a vague, ironic, recall of playing Cowboys and Indians as a kid. Yes, I did change my attitudes later. I grew up a little bit, I got some education, and this trip I am telling you about set the foundation for my schooling.

Black Eagle Dam to "Big Eddy"

It was a Monday, June 11, when we paddled on to confront Black Eagle Dam. Black Eagle replaces the original Black Eagle Falls, the last of the five waterfalls that Lewis and Clark encountered here in 1805. It was some 26 feet high when Lewis came on it and named it for a black eagle he saw in a tree on an island below it. Black Eagle Dam, built in 1890, was the first dam on the site. It was the first hydroelectric dam built in Montana; in fact, the first built on the Missouri River. This original dam was rebuilt in 1927. The reservoir behind it, only two miles in length, is called the Long Pool.

The dam itself is huge with a well laid out park and plant complex built by Anaconda Copper, which in most ways dominated the town of Great Falls at the time we were there. Anaconda and the other companies kept their properties in good order. Along both of the riverbanks were roads. Elcar chain-link fencing abounded. We began talking to a guard and Jerry got him to take our gear and canoe around the dam and out to the interesting little island below it. From here we launched into fast but easy to manage water. Shortly, we made it on down to the Giant Springs site[10] where we stopped for drinking water. This spring,

---

10 Lewis in 1805 said of Giant Springs, ". . . proceeded on up the river a little more than a mile to the largest fountain or Spring I ever Saw, and doubt if it is not the largest in American Known. . . has immensely Clear water . . . of a bluish Cast." Fred Bergson, ed. *The Journals of Lewis and Clark,* (New York: Penguin Books, 2003), 176. This spring flows 200 yards into the Missouri River and is recorded in *The Guinness Book of Records* as the shortest river in the world.

or cold water geyser, is unique and we were impressed and surprised by its beauty.

Leaving Giant Springs, launching out into the current, we were excited at the prospect of doing all of the dams in a day. Confidently, we paddled down to Rainbow Dam. Rainbow was no larger than its companions, but getting around it was vastly more complicated. Not far below it was Crooked Falls, so we had to portage both the dam and the falls at one go.

Figure 2.2 Crooked Falls

This was, as I wrote in my journal "a real bitch of a dam portage!" We had to carry the canoe and the gear a hundred yards, then lead the canoe along the bank over rocks and driftwood through brush tangles and willows. Then we portaged again around Crooked Falls, (well named to be sure) over more brush, rocks, parts of cars, and all sorts of debris.

We had a choice of routes at one point and Jerry went with the one I sized up as best—only it was a true ball-buster. At one point he stumbled and hurt his ankle badly. Stoic as he was about most things, and especially pain, he didn't make much of it. But I knew he was sore aggrieved. "That," he told me, "is the last time we'll take your route."

The truth is, both of our tempers were frayed by the exertions of dealing with various obstacles on this day. No pot of gold was waiting at the rainbow's end here.

Figure 2.3 Ryan Dam[11]

Still, as much of a hassle as it was to do the portage, our spirits rose when we hit the current below the dam and experienced the thrill of maneuvering past rocks and eddies. Unfortunately, it didn't take long to get into slack water again and very soon we came upon a concrete monstrosity looming ahead that shouldn't have been there—according to our map. This was a new dam, Cochran, completed two years before in 1960. We were surprised and thrown off a little. Nonetheless, things went better here. Improvising, we beached the canoe under one corner of the dam, climbed the near embankment, and grappled our gear and the craft up the face by rope to the top of the dam, deployed it down

---

11   This photo is courtesy of Google Maps, http://en.wikipedia.org/wiki/Ryan_Dam.

the other side, then portaged along the bank to the river. All in all this was slickly done. I'm sure Jerry was in pain, but he made no complaint, other than a few well-chosen cuss words.

The next dam was an hour or so farther on—Ryan. It was built on the site of the original Great Falls, which was a spectacular cascade. This dam is impressive in its own right. Bigger than Cochrane, it presented an enormous edifice of bulging concrete. We studied it for a while, then went looking for help.

Luckily, we ran into a Montana Power Company employee, Jerry Karr. He was a talkative man, friendly, and he readily offered to help us with his truck to accomplish this portage of several miles. He wouldn't take any kind of payment. On the other side of the dam, he helped us unload and as he drove off, gave a kind of heigh-ho! arm wave out the window. To this day I feel a great debt of gratitude to him.

Dams are impressive and overwhelming as you paddle up to them. But they are most beautiful and awe inspiring when you see them from below, from the downriver side. There is usually an amazing show of white water cascading down to the base, bursting upward, and rushing on over jumbled rocks. At Ryan there are two tiers, ledges of twenty to thirty foot falls just out from the base. The river flowing over them is a wonderful sight.

From the base of the dam, we shoved off for Morony, which, thank God, was the last and the easiest portage of the five, merely a double carry up the bank, then down again, not too far across, with easy access to the river.

And there before us it flowed once again—the unfettered Missouri River, tumbling over a series of beautiful rapids. Now there would be no more dams to worry about until we hit Fort Peck, one of the biggest dams of all. But Fort Peck was much, much farther on. We were just downstream of Great Falls, heading into the Missouri Breaks country, which would be about 150 miles of paddling through a rugged series of "scenic canyons and badlands." This, I was really looking forward to.

Jerry and I talked about the allure of the "Breaks," famous for its Badlands, and decided that we needed to celebrate a little. We pulled over to shore, unloaded a few things, and built a fire to heat up some bouillon. Jerry passed me the tobacco and both of us lit our pipes. It began to drizzle and I ignored it.

Having rested, helping Jerry reload the *Queen* so we could get back on the water, I saw a man and what proved to be his teenage daughter coming down from the nearby road, evidently to talk to us. As usual, we shared with them our adventures on the river and despite the light rain we talked until it became clear that either we had to disembark or they had to invite us to their place for shelter. They left, waving to us cheerily.

We shoved off then, heading into a course of rapids just ahead. Dutifully, we had scouted these rapids—in a cursory manner. Soon we were jouncing through waves much bigger than we anticipated, and after navigating an impressive hundred yard stretch, getting thoroughly wet and shipping a lot of water, we pulled over to the bank. The first thing we had to do was bail out the canoe. Next, we did another, more thoroughgoing, reconnoiter.

From the top of the embankment, we saw just how turbulent the rapids were. Still, both of us judged that they were not really that dangerous. It would be doable and exciting, if we could avoid the obvious jutting rocks and the shallows. This, however, was to be a day when we learned a lot about scouting rapids and how to judge the difference between how white water looked from the shore and how it actually was as you paddled through it.

Hardly had we pushed off, when the current caught the *Queen* and shot her through waves that broke over the bow. Whoa! Too late. From one moment to the next water splashed over my head, soaking me. Jerry caught water full front as well.

He was shouting instructions at me.

"Left, left, portside!"

"Watch that rock!"

"Head in to shore!"

At this speed, surrounded as we were with waves breaking around boulders on both sides, there was no way I could head us to shore. Nor was there any way to see disaster coming and avoid it. I was not thinking any of this, I was feeling it course through every fiber of my body. And the next instant we hit a rock, a big one, barely submerged beneath the swirling, white water. I pitched halfway over the *Queen's* bow and abruptly slammed back down onto my seat. Keeping a death grip on my paddle, I saw the boulder we were stuck on. It was huge. The canoe had rammed itself up about two feet onto it. For a tick we didn't move, just sat there with the water roaring past on both sides—the bow must have been a full six inches higher than the stern. The next second the rushing current began to swing us around. We were pivoting on the rock so that the stern swung out and down river, angling sideways. Feeling helpless, paddle poised, I sat there in the bow seat as we swung, sure that once we were fully broadside to the roaring current we would flip over.

Instead, in slow motion it seemed, we merely did a one eighty turn around the rock. We didn't capsize because Jerry in the stern, alternating his paddling between draw and J strokes, had maneuvered deftly to keep us upright. The canoe was still stuck on the rock, but now we were backward, facing upstream. Aside from our initial cussing, both of us were grimly silent.

Then I did the only thing that I could. I stepped over the gunwale onto the boulder. Standing athwart the bow, with one leg in the canoe and the other on the rock, I used my paddle to shove hard at the rock. We lifted and scraped free, off the boulder into its swirling back-eddy. Somehow I kept my balance and regained my seat and held on to my paddle. Then it was totally a matter of quick reactions and frantic paddle work. We straightened the canoe and plunged on down river—into the worst part of the rapids. What we had just negotiated was a mere warm up. In fact, just ahead was a steep descent, almost a falls, of perhaps four feet. As we approached it, I saw a channel to the starboard shore where the river broke around a small island and knew it was our best bet.

Jerry understood instantly what I was up to. We both pried at the water full strength and cut a beautiful, sharp angle across the rapids; the *Queen* had never handled better. Just as the worst of the rocks and monster waves came up, we veered into the shallows. Jerry jumped out and I followed. In our panicked attempt to beach the canoe or at least stop it, he tripped and fell. His ankle, already swollen from the previous day, somehow held up and he regained his footing, splashing forward to grab the gunwale. Both of us slipped and stumbled over the rocks, pulling the canoe and lifting it into what amounted to another portage, this time only a hundred feet or so, around to where a creek called Belt Creek emptied into the river.

Jerry was limping; we were both completely soaked, dripping wet. But, having made it to safety left us so relieved we had only had to look at each other to convulse with laughter. There was no discussion about setting up camp, we just did it.

Figure 2.4 Rapids below Belt Creek

Later, kicking back with pipe and tobacco, we let go of our earlier spat, and sat marveling over the hardships of the day and what we had managed to navigate. Neither of us were quite the cocksure voyageurs we had been. Later we would find out that mainly luck had saved us. We had barely missed being sucked into what is locally called, "Big Eddy." This phenomenon, referred to technically as a "special hydro-logic feature" is, as the nickname implies, an eddy, a very large one. It is created where Belt creek flows furiously into the river. The result-ing whirling undertow and turbulence are especially dangerous because boaters approaching from up or down river see them too late. Big Eddy has claimed several lives over the years, and even the Lewis and Clark Expedition found the eddy so difficult to traverse that they decided to camp just below it and they took most of the next day working their way up river past it.

We went to sleep that night too tired and too damp to really think about how close we had come, once again, to disaster.

The following morning, after a late rising and breakfast, we made sure to take our time scouting the rapids just below camp. The first order of business was to line the canoe by rope through the powerful white water created by the confluence of Belt Creek and the river. When this was done and we had come to the calmer section pictured above, we launched ourselves out into the river. The rapids here we had "charted." We knew by certain landmarks where the treacherous rocks and eddies were and what we needed to do to get safely past. We did fine work, shot on through, and made good time.

Jerry's Journal, Wednesday, June 13

A beautiful night. Got up late, ankle swollen; knocked it pretty hard. We are going through some great country. Tall white bluffs on both sides with varying strata, white clay on top with black layers to waterline—the falls and rapids caused mostly by hard red shale.

We stopped at a deserted homestead to have a look; about stepped on a rattler, both screamed, "snake!" and set the new world record for the standing backward broad jump. Mr. Rattler's hide is now mine, shot one time in the head. Dark mottling—shot another near a shed, over four feet, but he got away. Caught six golden eye, sort of slim silver carp-like fish, but with teeth—hits anything. Slogging through mud. Should make Fort Benton around five—cloudy, foreboding all day, now it rains. Omnipresent herons lead way—always on hills or flying or standing on shore. Beautiful. Would like to do wood statue of one. Saw some more geese. Came into town paddling a short cut—good day, all told.

Fort Benton to Virgelle Ferry

Thursday, June 14, we paddled the short distance into Fort Benton and pulled up to a boat dock near a park, part of a small museum complex. Upon changing clothes and washing up in the park facilities, we went into town and had delicious burgers at a place called Scott's, then a few beers at the Overland bar. All this time it was sporadically showering rain. As soon as we saw that it had cleared a little, we paid our tab and went out to find a place to camp. Deciding on a fairly secluded spot up on the levee, we had just finished staking the tent when the thunder and lightning rolled in. We ducked inside as sheets of rain whipped the canvas just over our heads. All night it rained. By morning the gear we had hoped to keep dry in the tent with us was soaked. We were used to being wet, but not having a dry change of clothes on hand was too much.

Having stowed most of the gear, we trooped over to the laundromat, loaded our duds in the machines and fed them coins. There was a bowling alley nearby that featured a little café and we went in for breakfast. The clothes weren't ready by the time we finished eating so, deciding to make the most of our wait, we walked over to check out the museum, which was just opening its doors for the day.

I had not realized the importance of the Missouri River to the settlement of the West until we looked at the exhibits and read the placards. Small as the town of Fort Benton is, it has a lot of historical significance. The American Fur Company had built the original Fort in 1846 and created a thriving business trading for bison robes with the local Indians, mainly the Blackfeet tribes. The fort had been abandoned in 1881 and all that is left of it now is the northeast bastion and part of one of the adobe walls.

During the1860s, the Montana gold rush days, the fort became the last port of call for the steamboats that plied the river. Travel up the lower Missouri had begun way back in 1819, but the first boats found the upper Missouri's currents and shoals so difficult to navigate that few ever made it past Nebraska, let alone to Montana. Regular river traffic beyond the Dakotas didn't develop until after 1860 when the *Chippewa* and the *Key West* docked in Fort Benton. This same year a Lieutenant John Mullan oversaw the completion of work on a trail that ran all the way from Fort Benton to Walla Walla, Washington, creating a route to the West that was much faster than the older trails, a route responsible to a large extent for the discovery of gold in Montana in 1862. Fort Benton became known as the Chicago of the plains. Evidently, the likes of Kit Carson and Jim Bridger had either lived in or passed through Fort Benton during this time and tens of thousands of miners and immigrants traveled what came to be called the Mullan Road.

Anyone who planned to travel the Mullan Road needed to get to Fort Benton first. They did this by steamboat. At times there were as many as forty steamships on the Missouri between Fort Benton and the mouth of the Yellowstone, near present day Williston, North Dakota. Men, women, children and livestock from points east in the U.S. and Canada, as well as half a dozen Indian nations, turned to the Missouri River steamboats for transportation and trade. After the Civil War, steamboats became a common sight on the Missouri. This was possible because of a new steamboat designed specifically for use on Montana's rivers. They were referred to as "mountain boats." A mountain boat had a shallow hull, ovoid bow, and broad beams. Approximately 140 to 170 feet long and 30 feet wide, it could carry 200 tons of cargo through waist-deep water. A veteran riverboat pilot like Mark Twain would have disdained even calling these boats "steamboats." He, of course, by this time, had quit piloting and was in California, writing a story about a frog jumping contest.

I tried to imagine a mountain boat on the river we were paddling and couldn't. Such a boat would be almost four times wider than those used by Lewis and Clark. Navigating the sandbars would have been a nightmare.

As we were leaving the museum to rescue our clothes from the dryer, two young boys fell in behind us. They followed us as we headed back with our packs to the dock and the canoe. While we loaded our gear, the two boys edged closer, wandering onto the dock to stare at us wide-eyed. It didn't take much encouragement to get them asking questions about where we had come from and what we had seen. Jerry was patient with this sort of thing. Though he never said as much, I think he considered it part of the trip, part of what it and we were about.

Watching the boys' faces as he spoke of the Gates to the Mountains and critters we had encountered along the river, I saw how we must look to them. Jerry's beard was thick and dark; he was looking more like a mountain man or voyageur every day; I was the tall, blond bearded, scruffy one. Maybe to the adults we met we looked like two bums, but these boys thought otherwise.

Generally, I got a kick out of hearing him elaborate on our "exploits," and hearing the odd questions that were often asked. Nonetheless, there were times when I just wanted to get underway. And this was one of them. It had turned into a beautiful day; I was eager to see the country downriver.

So I groused about how we needed to make some miles. Of course, Jerry agreed. But he kept talking. About all I could do was busy myself loading and arranging the gear in the canoe. By the time we got out on the water it was almost noon. I dug in, paddling hard, and said nothing.

Early on in our friendship we had come to some sort of tacit agreement to take each other pretty much as we were without complaint, though I always felt this came easier to Jerry than it did to me. But maybe not.

Our goal for the day, set earlier at fifty miles, had to be adjusted a bit. We would try to make Lippard, a very small town along the river, but one of our official stops for mail.

Going down from Fort Benton, the river often ran between steep, sparsely wooded bluffs. On top of the banks, back from the river were benches, plateaus that were miles wide, ranch land and wheat growing land, studded with more ridges and bluffs. I kept a sharp eye on the banks as we passed. In the days of Lewis and Clark we might have come upon bears. They had met with an amazing abundance of what they called "white bars," the huge silver tip grizzly, and complained that while the bears left the Indians alone they attacked their party at every opportunity. By the time of our voyage, however, most of the animal species they encountered were severely diminished, or, like the grizzlies, buffalo, wolf, and mountain goat, all but extinct. Otherwise, we were paddling through river country that hadn't changed much since Lewis and Clark, and I imagined that as little as eighty years before this we might have come on a band of warriors crossing the river on their way to hunt buffalo or deer and elk. Game had been so incredibly plentiful then. Living off the land had been an everyday reality, not only for the Indians, but also for white men after furs and those called woodhawks, who cut wood to sell to the steamboats, the people at the forts or small trading posts, or even to the occasional early ranchers in the area.

In my journal that evening I noted briefly: "Thinking of the old days." I was referring to the fact that after almost two weeks of virtually nothing but paddling, my movements in the bow had become automatic and my mind roamed freely, leading me places I had little awareness I was in until an inner image somehow drew my attention to it. I remembered being about nineteen, sitting in the waiting area of the tourist bus company for which I worked as a limousine driver between Glenwood Springs, Colorado and the internationally famous ski spa, Aspen, staring at a reproduction of a painting they had on the wall called, "Custer's Last Fight." I was fascinated by this painting and still am. Later, I found that this framed reproduction hung in almost any saloon I walked into. It was only after many years, though, that I learned it was painted by Cassilly Adams, and commissioned and distributed by a brewery, Anheuser-Busch. I think this one painting, this one ghastly, indelible image of the battle of the Little Big Horn, did more than anything else to create my sense of who the heroes of the West were and who the "bad guys" were.

Everyone knows that violence was endemic to the "settling" of the West. In the decades after Lewis and Clark's 1804-5 Expedition of Discovery, as trappers, farmers, merchants, and especially gold seekers, flooded the area, treaty after treaty was broken in flagrant land grabs and clashes between whites and indigenous peoples. From 1860 through the 1880s the hostilities reached a bloody culmination in The Indian Wars, as they are called. I imagined that right along the shores we were paddling past, settlers were burned out and slaughtered by raiding Indians. In reprisal whole bands of native peoples had been slaughtered. On top of that, since some tribes sided with the whites and others refused to yield, there was an increase in inter-tribal revenge killings.

Hindsight makes clear that Native American resistance to the encroachments of European settlers was tragically doomed from the moment Jamestown was founded in 1607. Apart from constant skirmishes, diseases introduced by European colonists slaughtered whole native tribal populations. The *coup de grace* came in1869 when through their advanced technology men of European descent were able to complete the continental railway. Native peoples, especially in the West, depended on the buffalo for food and much more. Completion of the Overland Route insured the virtual extermination of the buffalo from the Great Plains. Anyone who wanted to shoot buffalo could get on the train and do so. Shooting a buffalo from the window or the roof of a moving train car became great sport. Hide hunters killed eight million bison in a three-year period and left behind their stripped carcasses. As the meat rotted away, scattered piles of bleached bones remained and made the prairie so white that some said it looked as if it were covered in snow even in summertime. With the buffalo gone the Indian nations disintegrated into dependence on the Federal government. By 1890 most had been "removed" to reservations. I grew up in the West sixty years later, not even aware that I was part of a victorious culture, one that had "won the West," and at a price I had no way of understanding.

Paddling that day on the river, my mind slipped easily past such thoughts. The day, as I noted it in my journal, was memorable for the beauty of the steep bluffs and the tall cottonwoods, the willows and occasional pine ridges. I noted our animal sightings, especially muskrat, geese, and beaver. In fact, all along the way we kept coming across beaver sign and finally eased up on at least three in a one mile stretch of water, each of them greeting us with a loud tail slap.

Soon, at the top of a looping bend, we came to Brule Bar where we took a short break. Jerry, studying the map, said we had a stretch of white water ahead of us called Black Bluff Rapids, but from what he could see, running them without going ashore to do some scouting wouldn't be a problem. I agreed since on the map they looked to be hardly more than riffles, This, luckily for us, turned out to be the case. It was fun paddling the white water and easy to stay away from the rougher chutes.

All though this area there were many remnants of a bygone era of the West, some of which we knew about, but most of which we only learned of later. We knew as we passed a fairly large stream emptying into the Missouri, that it was the Marias River, and seeing it meant we had made 22 miles from Fort Benton. But we didn't know that Lewis and Clark had camped here and named the spot Decision Point because they thought the Marias might be the main fork of the Missouri and had gone up it for miles before deciding it wasn't. (Ironically, if they had followed it and gone across Marias pass they would have shortened their journey by two months.) Nor did we know that in January of 1870 the army had massacred a band of Piegan Blackfeet not a hundred yards from where we paddled. Over two hundred men, women, and children died in an attack lead by Major Eugene Baker, either shot outright or burned alive when their lodges were pulled down with them inside and set on fire. Neither Baker nor his men ever faced a court martial or any other disciplinary actions. However, since the Piegans slaughtered by Baker were a friendly band under Heavy Runner, rather than the hostile band just down the river led by Mountain Man, the public outrage over the killings did manage to stop the proposed transfer of control of Indian affairs from the Department of Interior to the War Department. President Ulysses S. Grant decreed that henceforth all Indian agents would be civilians and not soldiers. That led to a good deal of corruption, but at least henceforward Native Americans on reservations received more humane treatment overall.

As I said, though Jerry and I always looked for earthworks, for remnants that might indicate an old cabin or trading post, we knew nothing much about the local history. We knew that most of the islands we passed and certainly all the bends had colorful names given to them by either the Indians or early settlers and that the names probably figured large in local lore. When we did learn something, it was generally from talking to people we met at our stops for mail or drinking water.

At the Lippard post office we met an old man named Shane, who assured us we had no mail. He also said that he had never seen such a wet summer—the river was at its highest in sixty years. I still remember the grin that broke across his face as he said this. He winked and allowed he knew a whole lot more about the river than he wanted to know.

Things most people never had the misfortune to find out. He told us not to get out of our boat till we hit Judith River.

"Just keep your head down and go on past Virgelle Ferry and the Coal Bank and Little Sandy Creek, down to the Judith and camp there."

We nodded, humoring him. He was a wizened, hawk-faced gnome of a man and I didn't quiet know whether he was ribbing us or just plain addled. While he talked about "ol' Misery" and how deceiving "she" could be, I stood there gawking at the large gold nugget he wore chocker style around his neck. At today's prices that hunk of gold would be worth thousands of dollars.

A few miles down river, we came to Boggs Island near Virgelle Ferry and pulled in under a bridge to rest. It was threatening rain so we decided to camp nearby and make an early start in the morning. We were now heading much more east than north. This was rough sagebrush country, prickly pear country, but occasionally there was a pump house, so I knew the flats above the river were being irrigated. Right across the river I saw a cluster of white bee boxes.

As we sat smoking our pipes, the wind came up hard from the west, as though a door had been yanked open somewhere. Dark clouds were scudding toward us. We paddled a little farther on downstream and pegged the tent near a giant cottonwood tree. The gnarled tree had many gray, broken limbs and something of a foreboding air about it. Maybe it was because of the encounter with the old man, Shane, but I had a bad feeling about this place. All night the wind blew.

Friday morning, June 15, dawned windy, cold and rainy. Jerry did not stir and neither did I. His sleeping bag had gotten soaked somehow and my air mattress had sprung a leak. I had slept pretty much on the hard ground.

We got up, finally. I made the fire and Jerry made breakfast, then we shoved off. A cold, wind driven drizzle hit us as we paddled. Around 8:30, scorning Shane's warning, we stopped for supplies at the Virgelle Ferry mercantile store. Evidently, the town had prospered at one time. Just downstream was Coal Banks Landing, a large flat near the river that had been a steamboat landing. The Great Northern Railroad, as it was named at the time, cut right through town. Things must have been jumping for a while. But now it was virtually a ghost town. One of the handful of people left, the clerk, and I assumed owner, of the old mercantile general store told us we had made about 42 miles since Fort Benton and were 275 miles from Fort Peck Dam.

"Virgelle," he grinned, "is the last bit of civilization you'll see till you get there." He shook his head. "Where you're headed is called 'The Bad Lands'."

"Bad but beautiful, right?" I said.

"It's called bad for a reason," he replied.

Leaving, I tightened my wet poncho around me grimly and got back in the canoe. I was going to focus on the beautiful part, beautiful even in the rain.

An hour later the sky began to clear. There were puffy white, towering clouds along the horizon. We had gone north for a few miles, but now we were heading south and east. The river had quit its meandering. Straightening, it narrowed and the current quickened as we entered a deep canyon. There was Little Sandy Creek on our left and out in a wide flat, standing by itself like an Egyptian monument, I saw Haystack Butte, over 7000 feet in elevation. Soon the wide bottomlands disappeared and we were back in a canyon. Passing Eagle Creek, we saw huge layers of rock formed of black and white striations that created a thin wall of stone rising from both sides of the river. On the north it rose several hundred feet high and ran back into the sandstone bluff. The water changed speed as it charged past this wall. During countless ages, the river must have cut right through it. The water swirled and created wide sucking whirlpools, hissing and foaming against the boulders. Then we hit Kipp's Rapids. We had not expected them, let alone scouted them, but, luckily, they proved to be an exciting challenge rather than dangerous.

Just ahead were several famous landmarks: Eagle Rock, Citadel Bluff, and Cathedral Rock. The river turned northeast for five miles or so after this last formation and led us into a long series of sandstone spires known as the Pinnacles. They looked like toadstools 10 to 40 feet high. We passed the massive Steamboat Rock and soon afterward the Dark Butte and The Hole in the Wall. Of all the famous sites I have just named, the last was the only one we knew to look for at the time—and it was too far above us and back from the river to see. Nonetheless, hauntingly beautiful, grotesque rock formations surrounded us.

I have read that Captain Clark was particularly struck by this "White Castles" area. In his journal he noted, "A range of white cliffs—marvelous formations resembling columns, statues, and towers as if sculpted by the hands of some ancient, lost civilization."[12]

Captain Lewis is even more impressed, however, and writes:

> The hills and river Clifts which we passed today exhibit a most romantic appearance . . . The water in the course of time in decending from those hills and plains on either side of the river has trickled down the soft sand clifts and woarn it into a thousand grotesque figures . . . As we passed on it seemed as if those seens of visionary inchantment would never have an end . . . (spelling and punctuation are Clark's)[13]

Jerry and I were just as spell bound. Feathering our paddle strokes, we slipped silently along, admiring the beauty of the place. I began feeling much better than I had for days. All in all it was a wonderful afternoon of paddling. We saw pelicans, two deer, and made it unscathed through the Bad Lands canyon. Stopping along the way, we explored a little. Jerry took photos. Late in the afternoon we came to a cabin, a kind of river retreat, evidently. It was open to the world and stocked with food but no personal belongings. We requisitioned a few cans of grub, since we had run low, and left a note of thanks pinned to the door. We made our fifty miles that day just as we came out of the canyons into the big flat near the confluence of the Judith River. Here, by the ferry landing, we camped.

The Judith is a large river in its own right, ample and swift. As I learned later, Captain Clark named it for his lovely young cousin, whom he later married. He must have believed that if you feel you're the first of your kind to see a mountain, or lake or river, you are entitled to bestow

---

12   Fred Bergson, ed. *The Journals of Lewis and Clark,* (New York: Penguin Books, 2003), 146.

13   Fred Bergson, ed. *The Journals of Lewis and Clark,* (New York: Penguin Books, 2003), 143-4.

a name on it, like God naming the animals. Evidently, I unknowingly identified with Clark's impulse. That evening in camp, after we had eaten, I wrote a postcard to Gloria, whose middle name was Anne, a "report from the interior," telling her I had named a certain blue flower, rare and never seen before, after her, the *Glorianna*. This, of course, was not strictly speaking, true. But in any case, the card, for whatever reason, never reached its destination.

From the Judith River to Grand Island

The morning of Saturday, June 16, was overcast and nasty looking. We roused ourselves, ate, and then took some time to catch up on things that needed attention. Jerry cleaned and salted the skin of the rattlesnake he had shot at the abandoned homestead above Fort Benton. I patched my air mattress, congratulating myself for anticipating just such a problem. And, just as we were ready to hit the river again, the sun came out.

Lord, what a difference it made to paddle with the sun's warmth on my face and see sunlight shining off the water and reflecting off the willow leaves and cottonwoods. We stopped at Lohsi's Ferry to refill our water jugs and noted that the ferry approach jetty was gone, washed away—more testimony to how high the water was that spring. We had been traveling in the famous "Missouri Breaks" area for some time, and after leaving Lohsi's we passed through a canyon that must have been at least a thousand feet deep. I shouted back to Jerry that certainly we were passing Lewis and Clark campsites, and even Indian campgrounds. Several times we went to shore to look around at likely spots, but found nothing. I thought at one point I saw a bighorn sheep, but Jerry assured me they had been all but killed off. This was true in 1962, but today, through wise game reintroduction management policies, the Rocky Mountain Bighorn Sheep, as well as elk, have made a big comeback all through Montana.

We paddled down past Sturgeon Island, noting that the bluffs of barren gray clay that generally lined the river here didn't afford much of a place to camp. We began looking for another island and pulled into a large one on the south side of the river.

Jerry described the day's journey in his journal like this: ". . . paddled between high cliffs like hills round on top, falling to shear talus slopes. Mostly white and brown, broken and marbled as worn sphinx." Further on he says, ". . . saw a beaver sunning himself! Several deer, one who couldn't find our location because of our echo from a side canyon—kept looking there as we passed, unnoticed."

His last entry for the day was: ". . . rather uneventful paddle, though beautiful, but we made our fifty miles; tiring journey as the wind blew against us most of the afternoon. Should make backwaters of Fort Peck and a bath Sunday late."

This was not to be.

Disaster Strikes

Sunday morning, or to be exact, between 11 p.m. on Saturday the sixteenth, and 6 a.m. on Sunday the seventeenth, we lost our ride.

As I said, we had made camp on a large island, which we later learned was named, Grand Island. Hauling the canoe half out of the water up onto the island's sandy shore, we unloaded most of the gear, all except one paddle and both the life preservers, thinking that in the morning we would do some much needed cleaning and reorganizing.

The island was large, dotted with trees, mostly scrub cottonwood and willow. We set up our tent in a sandy flat of lush spring grass beneath a shaggy old cottonwood, made a fire, boiled up some tea, and cooked a little dinner. On this evening there were only a few dark clouds, rumbling far off on the western horizon. When night came, the sky filled with amazingly bright stars and the breeze was mild.

The next morning I got up first as usual. It was misty, fog hung low over the river, but seeing the sky was blue and clear, I rolled out of my sleeping bag readily, looking forward to a sunny day on the water.

That fantasy was short lived.

I scratched together some wood for a fire and put on the pan of rice Jerry had prepared for breakfast the evening before. I sang and talked to the kindling to encourage it to burn. As I coaxed the damp sticks into a full blaze, Jerry poked up out of the tent and took in the scene.

"Hell of a fog," he said.

He took a few steps toward the riverbank and stood stock still. A moment later I heard, "Where the fuck is the canoe?"

I turned and saw the *Queen* was gone.

Thus, began our closer acquaintance with the many reasons why people who know this river call it Ol' Misery.

I ran down to where the canoe had been. The grub box was there where we had stashed it. The canoe, however, was missing. I yelled exactly what Jerry had yelled. Both of us looked up and down the island's shoreline and across the channel.

"Well, son of a bitch," Jerry said.

And, of course, being Jerry, he shifted calmly into his analytic mode. He had a theory regarding what had happened.

"See how red and muddy the water is—and all these god damn sticks and crap along the bank? So, the water was clear yesterday, right? When we pulled in none of this shit was here. A cloud burst must have hit back in the hills during the night, flooded the ravines and gullies and they dumped all the runoff into the river. Christ, the water level is up by at least two feet—so the canoe just decided to float right up and take off downstream. Son of a bitch."

He was right as far as I could see, but far too calm about it to suit me. We were up a creek, literally, with one paddle and no canoe, out on an island—doubly marooned.

I walked to the end of the island and scanned both banks downstream for some hint of a long silver canoe and saw only willows and rocks. When I came back to camp, Deacon was standing hands on hips, staring out across the channel. A moment later, he turned and started rummaging around in the gear we had off-loaded the previous evening. He came up with the hand axe and some rope we sometimes used during portages, never imagining we would use it for anything else.

He didn't have to tell me his plan. We had been together twenty four hours a day for weeks and I knew what he was thinking—build a raft, get ourselves across the swollen river channel and find the damn canoe.

But first: food. I heated the rice, we ate, then set to work. Taking turns we chopped down four of the medium sized cottonwoods, lashed them together, and made a loose platform that might, in a pinch, pass for a raft. Most of the gear we stowed in the pup tent, a few necessary items we wrapped up and took along. Loaded up, we waded into the river, edged the framework of logs into the current, and then clambered aboard.

Immediately we were in water up to our waists—and the logs began pulling apart. Jerry was paddling with the one paddle and I was poling with a long tree limb, but we were making very little headway. We lost first one log of the raft then another. The raft, I decided, was not just a stupid idea in this swift water, it was a good way to drown.

I shouted something and Deacon yelled back.

We were heading down river fast. The channel we were trying to cross was like a chute. The raft, built in less than an hour, was about as stable as a one legged table. In the middle of the channel it flipped over. Now we were in real danger. Perched on the two logs that remained tied together, we bobbed along, scrambling to stay upright. Jerry was trying to paddle with one arm while I used my free arm to swim us shoreward. But we were heading past the far end of the island out into the river.

So, taking a chance, I lunged away from the splayed logs. My feet hit bottom. Jerry could see I wasn't going under and followed me in. Stumbling across submerged rocks, we struggled up on to the riverbank. Somehow we had managed to save the few things we carried, including the rope. Other than being thoroughly soaked and shaken up, we were okay.

One obstacle was overcome. Now, with a little luck we might spot the canoe hung up in some brush along the riverbank.

Jerry's Journal, Sunday, June 17

We hell bent down the stream to no avail—cursing for not tying off the canoe. Kicking through sticky gumbo mud and willows, finally, after five or six hours slogging came to a ranch. Was place owned by Perry Irish and middle-aged son

Dave. Peafowl and guinea hens in the yard, smell of hog profound in the air. Perry had a toothache—the rain had taken
out the road to town and the dentist there so he was dosing
heavy on aspirin. They fed us and Perry related Indian tales
and we actually ended up laughing a lot together.

Afterward, Dave drove us to Slippery Ann Refuge. There
was an office there. Just off the river. The Federal man at the
office took us to the DY Bar to call for an airplane search. But
the storms had taken out the phones lines along with many
roads. So he dropped us at Fred Robinson Bridge on highway
191 where it crosses the river. There we met Lupé Luna, quite
a fisherman and sportsman, had his wife and three kids with
him.

We talked, waited till he was ready, then piled into his old,
beat-up station-wagon. It had no shocks and we flat flew and
jounced the whole 90 miles up to Malta.

In Malta he introduced us to numerous people and really
he tried his damndest to get us a boat for a river search. His
own boat could not be reached due to high water. Jim Reeve,
a game warden, told us to come back in the morning and he
would try to get the Department plane to fly the river. Lupé
saw to it we were put up in a hotel.

Any Port in a Storm

This hotel, the Hotel Montana, was run by an older man named
McGruder. His hotel was really a kind of retirement home, catering to
long-term guests, pensioners. Lupé, after recounting our plight with a
few exaggerations for dramatic effect, had walked out the door. Now
McGruder was staring at us, shifting his considerable girth around on
the swivel chair behind the glass top showcase that served as a registration
desk. He had a game leg and made no bones about not liking to move
much.

"Yep," he said, "I think I have already heard about you boys. Ones
lost their boat on the river over near Irish's? Yes, yes, well, I do have

a room available. But it's payable by the week you understand, cash money."

Deacon and I exchanged looks. We had no real idea how long we would be trapped in this town, but, to me, paying for more than one night seemed to be the wrong move on several levels. I didn't want to encourage fate, for one thing. For another both of us were nearly broke.

McGruder, noting our hesitation, contorted his face sadly. His jowls quivered. His large, bloodshot eyes were those of a bereft bulldog.

"Hellation," he exclaimed. "Can you pay for *two* nights? Two dollars a night and a quarter extra for shower. And that means you can't expect no change of linens and towels, you understand?"

We nodded and in unison dug out the money. McGruder picked up the soggy bills with obvious distain.

"Son," he said, nodding toward me, "be a little careful where you lean yourself."

I drew back. He was talking about the showcase desk with its glass top, beneath which, on dusty green velvet there were spread innumerable relics of the Old West: two revolvers, some cartridges, a Bowie knife, cavalry patches, and even, as McGruder later vowed, a button off one of Buffalo Bill's shirts.

"Fine," I said, "but how do we register?"

He stared at me as though only the young and foolish would worry about such outmoded formalities.

"There's the guest register," he said, leaning forward to point down toward my feet.

I looked down and saw a scuffed leather bound book supporting a corner of the showcase.

"Hells bells," he added loftily. "Does more good where it is. Them pages is too brittle to take ink anyhow."

"And by the by," he added, tilting his head until his eyeballs all but disappeared under his bushy gray brows. "Same goes for the floors and walls of your room. Don't tromp and don't pound." He paused, eyeing us, then added, "Do you two fellers drink?"

Jerry grinned at him. "Hot as it is today? Damned right. What do you have in mind?"

"Oh, no," McGruder said, raising his hands and flushing slightly. "I'm T-total myself and only asking because if a man does maybe drink a little drop or two too much and starts to rough house up there in his room, stomping the floor and slamming doors . . ."

He grimaced, gesturing broadly around at the mounted trophy heads on the walls of the lobby.

"Hellation," he continued, "four years back a man fell out of his bed upstairs and it was enough to knock that ten point buck crack down onto the settee right there. Bang!"

He shook his head. "Lucky it was in the wee hours I tell you. Old Mike had been sitting right there on that settee all evening."

We both glanced around warily at the glassy eyed specimens and their huge dusty racks of antlers. "I take your point," Jerry said.

I laughed, but groaned inwardly, wondering just how in hell we had managed to end up here—and how were we going to get the hell out?

About an hour later, as I lay on the swayback mattress upstairs, contemplating our abysmal prospects, Jerry walked back into the room. He had been out somewhere chasing down a telephone so he could call his folks and let them know the latest. This was his first call home and I knew he had soft-pedaled our situation so as not to alarm his mother, Lois. I had no one to call, since both my parents were dead. Calling Gloria at the house she shared with others near campus would be chancy at best and besides I didn't want to worry her. It didn't even occur to me to call any of my immediate or extended family. My younger brother, Steve, was serving in the Air Force and my sister, Linda, was still in high school.

Deacon, amiable and talkative on most occasions, greeted me now with a grim look and slumped into the other major piece of furniture in the room, a balding Mohair chair by the window. He hadn't asked his dad for money, assuring him we had enough and if worse came to worse, we could hitchhike back. We talked it over glumly. There wouldn't be any hitching back home. That was just too humiliating a prospect to even contemplate. If we didn't find the *Queen*, we would hitch or ride the rails to the World's Fair in Seattle. It would be neat to see the Space Needle.

Jerry's Journal, Saturday, June 23

A lot of water down the river since last I wrote. We found out the next morning, Reeve couldn't help us out with an airplane search. He said if we didn't have any luck by Wednesday, he would take a boat from Havre. We tried talking to the Sheriff and other folk who seemed to be in a capacity, official or otherwise, to help us. No luck. Monday and Tuesday we laid around, left with Jim on Wednesday for Havre to pick up a state owned boat.

That same afternoon we were back on the island. It felt strange to be there, like visiting some kind of disaster site where everyone had vanished abruptly, with a pot on the grill, and pup tent still up, Croatan. We retrieved our gear in silence, all but the one paddle I had carried off to Irish's. Jim took us by their place and they had the paddle ready to hand over and insisted as well that we stay for dinner—ham and spuds.

We said goodbye to these hospitable men, father and son, whom we would never see again.

Thursday morning about eight we launched the search, me on one side of the boat, Rich on the other, and Jim steering and scanning both banks ahead, back and forth. The river is high and fast and has steep banks. All day we went downstream, staring expectantly and hopefully along the shore, using glasses and naked eye. Came to the wide bends leading to the beginning backwaters of Fort Peck Dam, and realized the canoe could be hung up anywhere among all the dead trees and brush. In the death forest marking the river's old course, checked many silvery drift logs, thinking maybe. But no. And so we camped for the night at the tail end of Fort Peck Reservoir on Fourchette Creek—in the rain. Friday we started back, getting more and more depressed about monetary loss, but much more over loss of face. "Who loses a canoe by not tying it up? How do you do it camped on an island?"

Now Saturday early, out of smokes, not watching for canoe any longer. Checking out the ranches, and so on, trying to decide whether to call Mom for money to fly the river— or not. No one saying very much.

Back in our depressing little room at the Hotel Montana that night, I thought of returning home. Maybe we should. Gloria would be glad to see me. It would be great to see her. Or would it? Could I really face her?

As we talked it over the choice became clear. We would head out for Seattle in the morning, hitch-hiking. This was an important decision. It boosted our morale. Seeing the World Fair wouldn't be New Orleans and we wouldn't have 3,800 miles of river behind us, but at least it would be an adventure.

Sunday, June 24, after our breakfast we were at the laundromat, clothes in the machines, sitting at a beat-up table, writing in our journals, when Jim walked in with his wife, Bernie, and their little girl.

He sauntered over, greeted us, introduced his family, then stood eyeing the two of us with the biggest grin in the world on his face.

"What would you say," he drawled, "if I told you I found your canoe?"

This was a moment of sheer joy. One I am sure that neither Jerry or I will ever forget.

Where the Hell *Was* That Canoe?

The map of Lost Canoe, Figure 2.5 shows Grand Island where we lost the *Queen* and our subsequent journey.

Three miles below the island, on the other side of the river, stood the Nygaard's ranch, a small place, difficult to get to, and at the time almost inaccessible. We had seen the house on the seventeenth, awhile before we came to the Irish's. For a time we stood debating whether to swim across and check it out. It looked as if the current from the island swept over against the bend in that direction. Still, it was hard to believe the canoe would be carried all the way across the river. We saw no hint of

sun glinting off aluminum. So we slogged on through the ankle deep
mud.

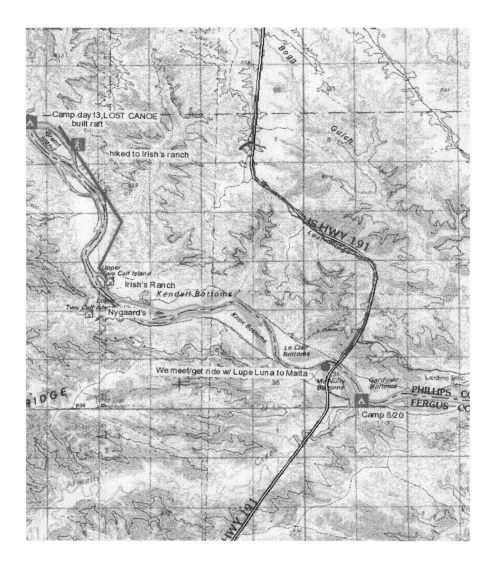

Figure 2.5 Map of Lost Canoe

Nygaard's ranch is rough looking, or was at that time. Essentially it
was a chinked log cabin with a sod roof that was obviously in need of

repair. The place was done in blue, as I remember, and the *Queen* was hanging in a shed off to one side. The shed, not far from the river, was used as a hog pen. I've told people that Bud Nygaard used the *Queen* for a day or two as a pig trough. That always gets a laugh, or at least a grin, but I'm not sure it's true. Bud did say he tried the boat out once himself and capsized it. That's when it occurred to him, only at that point, that since there was a paddle in the craft and two life vests and there had been such bad storms lately, maybe someone had run into trouble, maybe drowned. So he wanted to call the Sheriff—and would have except, as you recall, the phones were out due to the rains and flooding, down and dead until Wednesday. And we were on the river with Jim searching till Saturday. So, all in all, Bud did his best and no one could have been more appreciative then we were.

Jim helped us load the *Queen*. Jerry and I tried our best to thank him as we said good-bye from the riverbank below Nygaard's. He was one hell of a good man. After all, he did not have to lift a finger to help us—in fact, he suspected in the beginning we were poachers, out after beaver mainly, who'd had some bad luck. He had good instincts, all right. Nonetheless, he hauled us around, 150 miles by motorboat, 650 by truck. He did everything in the world that he could to help us in our plight, and finally he was the one who got the canoe back to us and saw us off down the river.

We were friends by then; that last evening in Malta his wife Bernie made dinner for all of us and we sat around till midnight, talking and drinking beer. Jim Reeve, stern on the outside, but generous, kind, and never hesitating to help others when he could, will always represent for me the true spirit of those people who live along the river.

III

THE BIG LAKES

Never were there two happier canoeists than the Deacon and I as we shoved off that day, Sunday, June 24. We had been grounded a solid week and were determined to make up for the lost time. The shoreline, the flood plains, and the occasional ranch we paddled past—they were all familiar to us.

By Monday we were down to the Musselshell River confluence near the big hairpin bend where we had camped with Jim on Fourchette Creek before giving up our search and turning around on the previous Friday. Passing the Musselshell, we found ourselves paddling among the copses, not to say corpses, of silvery skeletal trees that had been drowned by Fort Peck's backwaters. This was a somber place. We looked up to see cormorants, big and black, vulture-like, winging above the ghostly tree tops where they had built nests among the dead limbs. The day before we had come on several beaver, in the water and on the shore. Now I started and jerked around when I heard the sharp report of one's tail smacking down.

As we left the trees behind, the wind came up strong against us, creating waves even on that portion of the river where there was still current. We paddled till near eight o'clock and I was exhausted by the time we came to a shelter house near what was probably a commercial fishing guide's dock.

However, as we checked out the shelter, twenty by thirty feet maybe, open sided and with no ceiling, just a peaked roof and peeled pine trusses, lo and behold, we spotted cans of beer cached back under the eves among literally hundreds of empties. A six pack and two singles! My fatigue disappeared with the first gulp of Great Falls Select: *Miracle Cure.*

We set up camp that evening feeling as though our luck had definitely shifted. Full of confidence and with a few cans of Great Falls stowed away for emergencies, we headed out onto Fort Peck Lake—only a hundred miles to go to the dam.

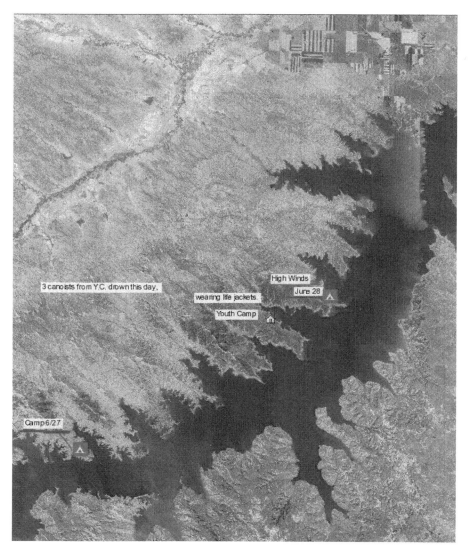

Figure 3.1 Fort Peck Lake

I don't mean to sound like we were being cavalier about taking on Fort Peck. But, realistically, you can't take it on, along with the next five dams after it where you'll be paddling vast, open waters for about 700 miles, without a bit of bravado. We had paddled Lake Sewell, Holter, and Hauser, and also the small backwaters of the five dams at Great Falls, but they were minor compared to what we were heading for now.

Fort Peck Lake pushes back 134 miles from Fort Peck Dam. It is remote and bordered by the 1,700 square mile Charles M. Russell National Wild Life Refuge. The fifth largest artificial lake in the country, it verges on the tribal home of several Native American peoples, largely the Sioux and Assiniboine. The water backed up by this dam is 200 feet deep in places and it has 1,520 miles or so of shoreline—this is longer than the coast line of California. If you look at an aerial or satellite view of the lake, as above, it looks like a giant millipede or Chinese dragon.

I prefer the dragon image.

Most books written about the Missouri River say it can be divided into three kinds of water and this matches our experience of it. We had already paddled the first third where the river runs wild and natural through beautiful country. True, these days it is commercialized by rafting companies and other ventures to some degree, but fortunately it is largely protected under the legislation establishing wild and scenic river areas so that generally it remains as it was when Lewis and Clark traveled it more than 200 years ago.

The final third of the Missouri's route begins below the last of the fifteen dams. It has been called the "Industrial Canal" segment because it has been engineered and dredged for river barge traffic and this has created an artificial channel; it begins at Sioux City, Iowa and runs down to the confluence with the Mississippi.

The second third, which we were now, on June 26, just beginning to paddle, is preponderantly made up of large lakes created by dams the Corps of Engineer's built for hydroelectric power and as flood control from the 1940s to 1965.

Each of these segments is beautiful in its own way, with its own wonders and difficulties, but this second segment, the seven hundred miles or so of slack water, was often times for Jerry and me a hell of sheer drudgery and dismal hardship. Looking back, I can say neither one of us ever considered calling it quits . . . except when we lost the *Queen* and didn't seem to have much choice in the matter. But Fort Peck Lake, water-dragon of the north, brought us close to the point of packing in our paddles.

To convey what we experienced during our voyage on this lake more personally, I will begin by quoting from our journal entries. I include photographs of the two journal writers. Below is a photo of Jerry taken about this time, complete with his ever-present pipe and regulation headgear, including homemade nose guard.

In my photo, which follows my journal entry, I had removed both sunglasses and guard for vanity's sake and to show off the hat Gloria had sent me en route.

Figure 3.2 Jerry on Fort Peck Lake

Jerry's Journal, June 26

This morning we headed out into the lake, some wind, but no white caps; it dispersed before long and we had smooth going. About noon I saw several huge paddlefish jumping, four to ten foot long. They looked like marlin with that bill on them. Told Rich but he didn't see them until one leapt as the boat neared, dove right under it. "Jesus Christ!" he yells, jumping up. "What was that?"

We landed near Hell's Creek, but on the south side because of the wind building up. During the night the wind gusted so hard we damn near lost the canoe again. We had it upside down on shore and the wind caught it, throwing it twenty yards, tumbling it into the lake—Zip Zap! Man, I was right on it—no more walking for me. Wind blew all night and I slept about two hours, holding that canoe rope.

Rich's Journal, June 26, 27, and 28

Tuesday: we hit a really beautiful day. Wind didn't come up until about 4:30. We camped, swam, fished, and had a good supper. The wind blew steady and came up fierce as we slept, throwing the canoe into the lake, though we had turtled it and had a rock on the painter. Jerry reared up out of his bag and charged splashing along the rocky shore after it, his backside gleaming in the moonlight. Quite a sight; I had to laugh.

The next day, Wednesday, we were forced to sit around camp—wind just too strong. I fished. At noon we started out across a bay, headed for a distant point of land, a sandspit. The lake shoreline is just one point of land after another, separated by wide bays, varying from a few hundred yards wide to several miles. Jerry charts as straight a course as possible from one sandspit to another, but we have to beware of getting too far out on open water. If there is any wind at all, and most of the time there is, white caps spring up and waves at least three feet high. The bays, which of course, before the dam was built, would have been long gullies or ravines, can be very deceiving—what looks like an hour paddle can easily be twice that.

Today, just past 4:30, wind eased off. We made a very long haul at dusk across vast stretch of water that was smooth, without a ripple, beautiful with the setting sun reds and oranges reflecting in it. Not a boat, not a soul, anywhere. The entire world was just a peaceful dipping of our paddles and the occasional bird flight. Next morning, Thursday, started off strong, but the wind swooped down, slapped us with three to four foot swells and we almost didn't make shore. That day we sat on a sandspit, watching the wind make waves until evening calm hit. Made maybe ten miles.

Figure 3.3 Rich on Fort Peck Lake

Jerry's Journal, June 27 and 29

Wednesday. Too windy to start. We got underway about 11:00, across to north side and then to an island where we waited for the wind to die down, then did a diagonal to south side where we waited for storm to pass. I shot a carp and caught (snagged) a golden eye and beat Rich at gin. We made it for the north shore and finger of land and got there at sunset. Fried up the carp for dinner—bad (soft and boney). Wind came up strong in the night. Hope for good weather tomorrow. Only forty miles to go.

. . . Thursday it was blowing hard all day until 4:30 when we paddled across an inlet to a sand tip, but breakers and waves became just too big; sitting now how many hours on these points of land? Flooded by dam and now receding the water reveals earth barren of plant/animal life, just gumbo clay and rock chips. We left this north finger during evening calm and paddled past Pines Recreation Camp till dark, after nine.

This morning, Friday June 29, calm and after a good paddle we made the dam by 10:00. Fort Peck Dam is big, higher than Canyon Ferry, must be over 250 feet. Washed canoe and ourselves, walked around, took some pictures, several men stopped to talk to us and take our picture. We accepted kind offer from two fishermen to tow us around dam, bought supplies and got mail and money. Also, chillingly, learned 10 Boy Scouts from Recreation camp we passed capsized canoes and four drowned out in big waves with their life jackets on—as we sat sulking on sandspit. We were underway by 4:30. Then got stopped by wind. I watched a bull snake along shore, drinking, flicking tongue, stopped after very short drink, just left lower jaw under water. I caught him, almost five feet long; thinking of Betty's pet garter snake, I let him go. We paddled on for six miles or so and made camp in a wind storm on a sandspit; too worn out to even put up tent; slept out and got soaked.

Figure 3.4 The Weather[14]

On the river weather controls your life. At the beginning of our voyage, I was used to thinking of nature as the Great Outdoors, a place one goes for recreation. Going camping or fishing or climbing—these were all ways to have fun. I suppose on a deeper level getting away from civilization and the fetters of society gave me a sense of authenticity. I could experience myself for who I really was and life at its most compelling and genuine. I had read Jack London's "To Build a Fire" and seen movies dramatizing the idea of "Man against Nature." But the notion had no real meaning for me.

This changed after that first battle with the waves on Canyon Ferry Lake. I found that in the mornings when I rolled out of my sleeping bag and saw the sun rising over the horizon into a clear blue sky, I felt elated and blessed. If it were cloudy, if the wind were blowing, my spirits sank and I cinched my dwindling supply of resolve a little tighter, and got up. During this stretch, it rained or soaked us with sporadic showers for days at a time.

---

14 Photo taken by Bill Shirley, property of Jerry Sanders.

On the water in a canoe you are at the mercy of the weather; it plays with you, dominates you. The wind, even if it is quiet, slumberous, often wakes abruptly and begins to howl; it is always poised to spring some new attack on you. Often it seems like a trickster spirit, cunning and malicious, lying in wait, pouncing when you least expect it and are most vulnerable. It allows you a day, or even two, of fair passage. Then sneers and pummels you with six kinds of misery. You try to be stoic about it. After all, you know the first sin of the outdoorsman is to take the weather personally. You learn quickly, if you're smart, that taking your feelings out on your gear or your partner solves nothing and makes things worse. Still, as time passes it gets harder to avoid feeling irked at how it is treating you. Inwardly you fume and despite all your rational resolve become superstitious. It's not surprising that long haul canoeists, like the early voyageurs, revert to the old ways. The weather gods must be, will be, respected, placated. Maybe you don't consciously think up and employ a pattern of invocation and supplication of the river gods and the wind and the powers lurking back in the fog along the shrouded banks. But you grow wary, brooding over certain shifts in the wind, the look of the lake when long tongues of wind-riffle cross it, the mist in certain coves, odd spoor along the shore, the long S curved trail across the sand beside your tent, leading to the water and not returning— snake.

Why do you find a piece of wood that looks right and throw it just so into the fire and watch carefully as it burns? Why do you make a little pile of rocks near camp and put a found feather on it? And this anxiety that nags you about these little rituals you and your river partner have— which of you does what and how it's done and in what order—what is that about?

A woman you love is waiting for you, but gradually your longing for her becomes sporadic, you find your thoughts of her have become foggy, reduced to something like a worn photo that vaguely signifies home. The next paddle stroke, the far point of land you are headed for, the mood of the weather—this is all there is. There is only the sense of being out under a vast, indifferent sky, in the middle of miles of water, sand, rocks, clouds and wind—nothing else means anything.

Fort Peck Dam to Williston, North Dakota

As Jerry noted in his journal, we made Fort Peck Dam and camped below it Friday night, June 29. This stretch of the river below Fort Peck, heading west and angling south toward Garrison Dam, nine, maybe ten days away and across the Montana border into North Dakota, was tough—mainly because of the weather. To quote Jerry again, "Now it is Saturday and we made Oswego, but the wind is pushing up big waves. All the way down from Fort Peck, meandering and bends. Saw the remains of a stern-wheeler ferry—*Faith Ferry*—dangling in water. I am depressed, muscles and joints hurt, damned air mattress went down again."

Remains of *Faith Ferry*, eh? We made jokes about this. We still had our sense of irony—and our sense of mission. But the long hours and days of this first month on the lake had worn away the spirit of adventure that had carried us through the early weeks of paddling. We had hardened a little physically and also mentally. It helped that we were in territory that was relatively "new" to us both, which made it more interesting since we didn't know exactly what to expect. This was reservation country, mostly the Sioux and Assiniboine peoples, the ninth largest reservation in the United States, a separate nation, though few people think of it in that way.

In the next several days we made Wolfe Point and then Popular, where the Fort Peck Indian agency is located. We walked into both these river towns for supplies, especially water. At Wolfe Point I started off for town alone. As we came down river into more populated areas, we had become wary of leaving the *Queen* unguarded. But an old fellow, an Indian man fishing nearby, put down his pole and called out that it was too far to walk and offered to give me a ride in his pickup. It was parked a ways off, up a dirt trail. He said nothing until we got in the truck, then began to question me about our sudden appearance. He was a little incredulous, I think when I told him all about our voyage. In town he let me off at a grocery store, shook my hand, and drove away, waving and honking. Later, having bought what we needed, I was lugging the paper sacks of food and beer and water toward the river when another pickup slowed and the driver invited me to climb aboard. I was happy to get a ride the rest of the way. The men in back with me were generous with their beer, grinning and friendly. We jounced along the road and one guy kept looking at me. He said something to another man who laughed. I couldn't understand the words. The second man shrugged and said. "You look like . . . eh, Nature Man, man."

Nature Man? I asked again what that was suppose to mean, but he shook his head. "It's good, man," he said. "Sort of a compliment."

Everybody laughed and I joined in. Something, I assumed, and who knows what, was lost in the translation. They were amused by an Anglo who looked like a bum or Beatnik. Or they felt some kind of kinship. In my journal I later wrote. "Those guys were nicer to me than anyone would have been in my own hometown. What a gas."

Sitting on the riverbank near the canoe, Jerry and I tore into a six-pack. A few beers later we decided, what the hell, we needed to go into town—together this time. I had forgotten to check at the post office for our general delivery mail.

The fisherman, still there, told us not to worry. No one would bother our gear. We walked in, cleaned up and ate. At the post office there was no mail for us; we hadn't realized it was Sunday. Nonetheless, we jotted several postcards apiece and dropped them in the slot. Jerry phoned his family from the public phone booth there.

Thinking we would have a last beer and get back before it got too late, we dropped in at the Montana Bar. It was open. Or was it? Unfortunately, the barkeep was out of commission, too drunk to pour. Patrons seemed to be just going behind the bar to pull their own. I was tempted to follow suit, but no one encouraged us to do so and after sitting, taking in the scene for a while, we made our exit.

The fisherman nodded to us as we came out of the trees and down to the boat launch pier. The *Queen* swung gently at the end of her tether. We exchanged weather talk with the old man. The sky was clear. Was it going to rain tonight?

He nodded his head. "Damn right!"

We paddled off and made it several miles, past a bridge, before the wind came up. Very soon the sky grew black. That night all-jolly hell broke loose; we had camped in the trees, hoping for protection from the coming storm. Evidently, the swarms of mosquitoes, which Deacon called "pesky wickerbills," and "bloody o-skeetos" were of the same mind. Our repellant did not impress them one wit. As we slapped and cussed inside the dark pup tent, the sheets of rain slapped us time and again. We were strobed by lightning for hours. The tent could not withstand such driving rain; wherever we touched or lay against the canvas, water soaked right through.

In the morning, scratching mosquito bites and wringing out our wet gear, we skipped breakfast and got underway, planning to eat something in Poplar. We tied up somewhat below the public boat launch area so that we would not have to worry about the *Queen*. This meant that in order to get to town, which was farther back from the river than Wolfe Point, we had to traipse through a marsh and dump area. In town it seemed that we kept encountering the remnants of a big weekend party. Maybe the ritual here was to celebrate the Fourth of July ahead of time, a kind of Native American protest celebration? We never found out an answer to that one.

In any case another pickup truck load of Indian men offered us a ride on the way back. We talked to them for some time. Jerry, in his journal, notes that one man in particular was talkative. "He repeated several times he was in the Army for five years, seven months and twenty eight days. He sounded proud of this fact, but also resentful, if not angry."

The next day, Tuesday, having been relatively free from mosquito attacks during the night, we were off early, hoping to cross into North Dakota by evening.

The rain jumped us about noon. I remember this as a real Black Letter day. The rain was hard and cold and steady. We saw an abandoned car; a '51 Ford, half in the water under a bridge, and, tying up next to it, got in the back seat, out of the rain.

Four hours we sat in that hulk. Off and on both of us dozed; I saw a small brown bird come and go through the broken windshield. It must have had a nest in the car's torn ceiling liner. Out it would fly; ten minutes or so later it was back. I sat perfectly still in the gloom, waiting, watching. The only sounds were Jerry's slow breathing, the rain hissing into the river, and the occasional flutter of wings. The rain kept falling.

We were barely a month out of Three Forks and it seemed we had been on the river forever.

Williston: Sunday, July Fourth

Making it to Williston, North Dakota was a definite milestone. For one thing we were finally out of Montana. From here on we would be paddling southeast, angling down for our confluence with the Mighty Mississippi. A few miles farther on out of Williston, we would hit the slack water of Garrison Dam. After Garrison . . . only four more dams to go.

The evening of the third, we had pulled in late and set up camp on a level spot between the water and a sheer concrete wall—this site, as we discovered when we walked around a bit, was part of an abandoned coal mine. We woke to mist and fog, and, as Jerry noted, "Both of us looked automatically for the canoe." Once again it was there, tied and double tied.

Setting out early, paddling hard, we made it by noon across the border and into North Dakota. The sun came out and our moods improved.

At noon we drifted awhile, sat out on the water, eating fruit and crackers, drinking juice. Then we dug back into our paddling, determined to make Williston. Suddenly, Jerry yelled out to me, "Wait! This is not the right river!"

Not the right river? I gazed around and realized what he was talking about. We were heading up the Yellowstone.

We had been tricked by the fact that here, at the point of its confluence with the Missouri, the Yellowstone was the bigger of the two rivers. With the wind blowing there was no way to tell the direction of the current. Laughing at ourselves, happy to have made it to the Yellowstone, we backtracked and continued heading toward Williston, which now we knew was close by. We stopped for water at an irrigation installation of some kind and found three or four people to talk to, mostly about the weather; then paddled on, docking along a deserted stretch of the river bank just below Williston.

We debated whether to go in, since it was a holiday, but really we had no choice. We were out of repellant, though we had just bought a supply. No way were we going to spend another night at the mercy of the wickerbills if we could help it. There had to be a gas station open that would stock bug spray. The walk into town was a long one. It was late afternoon and we were hot and thirsty. The first place we came to had the old fashioned name of The Idle Hour. The barkeep was a large man, bald and with mutton chop sideburns. We had barely taken a seat when someone asked what we were up to. Soon the patrons' celebration of the Fourth became mixed up with celebrating our journey and we had more free drinks than we could handle. At some point a man named Elmer asked if we wanted him to drive us into the business section of town, fearing, evidently, that we would get lost walking in on our own.

He dropped us off, and we found a café that was open, had our dinner, and headed back toward the river. Of course, we had to stop again at The Idle Hour, if only to thank the barkeep for his hospitality. Elmer was there and had been joined by his stepson, Jim, who insisted we all hoist another. I don't think I ever enjoyed a night of talking and joking and putting money in the juke box more. It was past midnight by the time Jim drove us back to camp.

And too late I remembered we hadn't bought the mosquito repellent.

Lake Sakakawea

The addition of all that water from the Yellowstone River had widened the muddy Missouri considerably. Shortly after we left Williston, as we came into the slack waters of Garrison Dam's reservoir, Lake Sakakawea, it grew even wider. At 178 miles long, Sakakawea is 14 miles across at its widest point. The country around the lake is flatter than that around Fort Peck, so there are not as many drowned ridges and rocky spines reaching up out of the water. The shoreline, 1,300 miles of it, is more regular.

I had thought that this might mean we would have easier going as we paddled toward Garrison Dam. But I didn't factor in the increased momentum of that wind sweeping across the open plains and wide lake waters. Ever optimistic, I had reckoned that most of the water in the heavens had already been dumped on us. It couldn't get any worse. Yet it did.

The saving grace about our time on Lake Sakakawea was that the trickster gods of the river relented to the extent that after a day of brutal wind and rain, we would generally have a gorgeous day of warm sunshine, clear blue sky, and calm. Early rising, never a strong point with us, was part of the pact we made on the morning we set out from Williston. We vowed that rain or shine we would be up and out there by . . . well, at least eight a.m.

Whatever it took, we would power our way down the length of Lake Sakakawea in less than a week. Fort Peck reservoir had almost done us in, at least in terms of our morale. We weren't going to let that happen again, regardless of the wind or the rain. So each morning we ate a big breakfast and topped it off with pancakes and syrup and set off.

Stopped by wind, we waited it out in a cove. These "layovers" didn't seem too bad by now. During the last weeks we had become more tolerant of being grounded this way. We fished, played cards, swam, reorganized our gear, wrote in our journals, and read. Once the wind died down, we were back in the canoe. We tried to average ten hours a day paddling. The afternoons and evenings stretched on and on. It didn't get dark until around nine thirty so we usually kept at it till at least eight o'clock each evening. The coves we camped in were actually secluded inlets, tucked away between granite outcroppings where we were protected to some degree from the wind. There would generally be a sizable patch of more or less level sand or grass on which to set up the tent. We no longer worried about whether the wood around camp would be wet or dry, we could get a fire going regardless, but it was nice to have it be as abundant as it was now.

We saw very few watercrafts on the lake that I recall. Occasionally, we saw a fisherman, and the day we reached the confluence of the Little Missouri, one of the larger tributaries of the Mighty Mo, we met a fisherman named Jake Stark, who proved to be eager to hear about our trip and provided us with the name of a relative of his who might be called on to give us a ride into Mandan later on.

For the most part, however, we were alone; we were surrounded day after day by nothing but water, low bluffs and hills that stretched away to the far horizon. The feeling of solitude was profound.

On Sakakawea we experienced truly wide and open water. This was uncommonly beautiful and it also meant that navigation was tougher, and even perilous. In order to avoid wasting time and energy, Jerry picked our headings carefully. Several times this meant making really long hauls, as opposed to Fort Peck where we would shoot from one ridge spur to another and always know where we were.

One afternoon as we paddled blithely along out in the middle of the lake, several miles from either shore, hardly aware of the wind, we found ourselves gradually overtaken by rollers at least four feet high. Overtaken, as in—the wind was blowing *down* river. This was something it rarely did. Pushed over open water by the wind from miles upstream, the waves were coming in under us from behind. For a while we rode the swells, enjoying the novelty of the back-arching, undulating, bronco ride movement and the sense of speed. Soon, though, that bronco was sunfishing, we were pitching up, down, forward, and back—vigorously—and decided to head in. It was great fun while it lasted.

Another day on Sakakawea we beached on the south shore about noon, had our lunch, finished it up with lemon juice and a smoke, then set out for a point on the north side that looked to be eight miles or so away. It was a glorious day, bright water, calm.

We paddled steadily for two hours. But something wasn't right. I felt it and looked across the lake to see that the shore ahead was no closer than it had been when we started out. Glancing around at Jerry, I saw that he had become aware of this too and had begun consulting his map.

The wide-angle crossing we were making that had looked to be eight miles was at least twice that. We considered angling back toward the shore we had come from, but that would have been just as dangerous as continuing on our present heading, dangerous because if the wind came up and caught us out here, we had a good chance of capsizing and if we didn't we'd have one hell of a fight on our hands to make any shore at all.

We kept paddling, not talking, saving our breath. The calm held and we reached the far point after a long and intense three hours of paddling. We had done a straight shot of twenty miles pretty much down the center of the lake. Beaching the canoe on a sandspit point, we both eagerly examined the map, thinking surely the dam must be right around the bend. But our excitement was short-lived. No matter how hard we looked at the map's contour lines, it was clear that once we passed the bend it was many more miles to the dam.

Garrison Dam

Nonetheless, when Garrison Dam came into view around 10:30 Monday morning, I felt a definite sense of elation. We had left Williston on the fifth and we were heading in to portage Garrison on the ninth. In other words we made it down the length of the lake in about five days, averaging close to forty miles a day. After beaching the canoe, we walked to the power station to see about getting a ride. Garrison is a big place. The dam is 210 feet high, smaller than Canyon Ferry and Fort Peck, but not by much. At the time it was studded on the outside with pinkish rock, 60 feet wide at the top and incredibly long: almost two miles.

In the power station, we were told we needed to take an elevator up to a company office. At the elevator, a man stepped in with us and Jerry struck up a conversation with him, asking him at some point if he knew of someone who might be able to help us with our portage. He thought about it a tick or two then officiously said he really didn't think there was anyone at the dam who could help us. A moment later the elevator stopped at what was evidently his floor and he stepped out, disappearing without a word. This was the first time we had been stiffed by anyone working at the dams. Usually, we were welcomed pretty heartily, at least once it was clear what we were up to. Many sportsman and water enthusiasts used the lakes and enjoyed various activities on them, but how many were on a 3,800 mile canoe trip and wanted to portage from one side of a dam to the other? Workers at the dams, and especially Corps of Engineers employees, always wanted to question us on what we had seen and how our trip was going.

That didn't seem to be true here. Still, it wasn't too long before we came across a Corps employee who liked to talk. He ended up giving us a tour of the powerhouse. There were five turbines, etc. This sort information I could have easily looked up if I cared to and I didn't. More interesting was a detailed diorama of the entire system of fifteen dams. We spent some time here, looking it over, since it gave us a strong visual rendition of how far we had come and how far we had to go.

We also came across information about Garrison Dam that is just as interesting to me today, if not more so, as it was then. Garrison was built in Indian territory, on the Fort Berthold Indian Reservation, the home of the Mandan, Hidatsa, and Arikara nations. Fort Berthold, named for an early army fort in the area is over nine hundred thousand acres, yet it is only a remnant of the twelve million acres that were deeded over to the Native American people in the Fort Laramie Treaty of 1851.

When Garrison Dam was completed in 1956, just six years before we paddled it, the Missouri's waters slowly piled up behind it and over the top of three towns on the reservation. They were drowned, along with farmlands that had provided the Indians food and livelihood for centuries. A way of life was lost forever.

I had no way of knowing for sure, but as I read this information, I felt Jerry and I had paddled directly over the corpses of those towns on the previous day.

Jerry's Journal, July 10, Washburn, N.D.

A man named Eddie Frankie stopped to talk to us. He wanted our names for some sort of log that was kept of river travelers. In return he gave us and our canoe and gear a ride into Riverdale for supplies, waited for us, and then drove us down to the river below the dam. It must have been about noon by then. Rich and I were in no hurry. We drifted through some deep green cold water coming from the tailrace below the dam. Slow current, there were many white sandbars here. The river banks were covered with heavy undergrowth, the draws filled with choke cherry trees, junipers, lots of berries to eat, bramble patches; the bottoms along the river were weedy, with tall cottonwoods and sandy shallows. Lots of deer sign. Back on the lake we saw a paddlefish jump—small one about eighteen inches, semi-transparent, its bill longer than its head. Very primitive looking fish. We've come on many white tail deer. Two traipsed through camp in the night. The last two days the weather has been great. We wear only shorts. Of course, the mosquitoes are back in force, but thanks to the package from the folks we have now rigged a mosquito bar, sleep good. When we are on the water—no bugs.

I am beginning to solidly enjoy this type of life—except for the wickerbills. We went into the little village of Washburn, S.D. Giggling waitresses, Black Label beer, people on street eyeing us, suspicious of two bearded, shabby, river rats, wearing cardboard nose shields.

Then we floated two and a half hours. Drank & sang. Rich jumped overboard and right back in boat. Water still cold. Saw badger coming down for a drink—couldn't get a picture.

Rich's Journal, July 12-14, Fort Yates, N.D.

Caught 3 pound yellow belly catfish—made a very good breakfast. We pushed hard, 75 miles today. This was after slack day yesterday when we went into Mandan, docked at the Reichert Marina and hitched a ride with a furniture salesman, who had gone to school in Europe for a year, he said, and waxed on about his desire to make a river trip too. Seems to be a common theme of men we meet. They may be stuck in a boring job for the time being, but they are just waiting of the day when they have the money to break out and go adventuring. We washed our clothes and picked up mail. I received a sad, moody letter from Gloria. Judging by his silence, Jerry didn't fair much better in the news from home category. I always envy his mail—his mom writes a lot, and Betty, even his friends occasionally.

We didn't go into Bismarck; paddled hard and made Fort Yates and camped on a sandbar just above; it is the town where Sitting Bull was killed, so a fisherman told us. "At least his grave is here," said the fisherman. "Some bastards from Mobridge tried to steal his body, but he's here all right, buried under concrete. They just dug up horse bones. We have a monument to him."

I am very tired tonight. The only thing I know about Sitting Bull, aside from the fact that he was one of the greatest Indian leaders, is that he left the Buffalo Bill Wild West Show for home, saying, so it's said, "I would rather die as an Indian than live as a white man." We saw another badger near camp.

Figure 3.5 Abandoned House

July 14. Worse day yet—rain all day—made one mile. It was bad yesterday when we hit wind as we came into the slack water to Oahe Dam and seemed to paddle in place for hours—made eight miles. But today . . . we have been forced to find some shelter away from river and are now sitting out the wind storm and rain in this abandon house. We waded through knee-deep water to get here—an eerie place. Half of the floor gone in this room—you can look down into the dark of the cellar. Something splashes around down there. A rat, I figure, or several, a posse of rats. Cheery thought, since we will sleep here tonight if the storm keeps up. Jerry just now pointing out the swallows. They are building a nest in the other room and fly by, orange streaks, shiny blue-black. To me this is a cowboy version of the House of Usher.

Into Mobridge and on to Oahe Dam

We were officially in South Dakota now, on Lake Oahe, which begins in one of the Dakotas and ends in the other, smack up against Oahe Dam. Ahead, we had eleven more states to pass "through" before hitting New Orleans, not that we were counting. We had enough on our minds just dealing with the wind and rain on Oahe. At one point we had camped on an old dirt road bed. The tire ruts were grassed in so the spot was pretty flat; it seemed ideal as a tent site. And it would have been, except for the storm that rolled in during the night. It rained so hard that the road, which was on a slight slope, became a creek and the water flowing in one end of the tent carried my air mattress—and me on it—right out the other end. This must have happened slowly. All I know is that I woke up near dawn several feet down the road with nothing but gray sky over my head.

Somehow, Jerry's air mattress, though it had been lifted at least an inch, stayed in the tent and his sleeping bag was dry. He thought the whole thing was very funny.

"Hell, of a good sleep." he said. "Always wondered what a waterbed would be like."

Luckily, the sun came out at mid morning. By evening my bag and clothes were reasonably dry. My spirit, however, was soggy. I was in a foul mood, brooding over the wet hen smell of my sleeping gear, the urge to claw my raw chigger bites, my river partner taking one stroke to my two, and the injustices of life in general. In particular, I hadn't gotten any mail from Gloria at our last stop and I had begun to wonder what was really at the bottom of her last moody missive.

I glean some of these memories from my journal entries, others from Jerry's, but I still remember clearly how I felt on Lake Oahe, the longest, at 210 miles of all the lakes we paddled. It was near the middle of our voyage. The mountains were far behind us, and with them, the truly interesting "scenic" sections of the river, or so I thought.

We were heading south and east, just passing out of Oahe's upper end slack water, not far from Mobridge, South Dakota. Again we found ourselves paddling through trees up to their waists in water. At first they had leaves; they were dying, of course, and the leaves were yellow or crimson. It was like we had gone suddenly from summer into autumn. Paddling on, we came into trees whose uppermost branches, barely above the water, naked and skeletal, were perfect nesting places for the reptilian looking cormorants.

Figure 3.6 Slack Water Trees

There were times we were thankful for these trees because we could find no firewood, not even wet stuff, and we had to paddle among them, breaking off branches, some of which were always dry enough for fuel. But generally, as on this day, paddling through the dead and dying tree-tops cast a gloomy mood. When the last of the them disappeared and the vast ghost communities of drowned trees were out of sight beneath our keel, we moved out onto open water with a feeling of relief.

Still, even though we were now out on the wide and beautiful lake the despondency that had begun during the night in the dismal house nagged at me. It became difficult to fight off.

All I could do was focus on what was ahead. We had three dams to go after Oahe, then we would make good time down to Sioux City.

The middle section of the voyage was, in terms of mood and motivation, the most difficult part for me, and, I suspect, for Jerry as well. Each day for many hours I did nothing but sit in the bow of the *Queen* and paddle, stroke after stroke. The banks of the river and the landscape we were passing through held little novelty. Aside from attending to immediate concerns like sandbars and floating driftwood, my mind was either simply *there*, oblivious to anything but the present moment of water and paddle movement, or idling in neutral as the same quotidian thoughts cycled through it. I didn't want to be just goal oriented, numbing myself out thinking only of "getting there," off somewhere daydreaming, spinning a fantasy of future satisfactions and missing out on what was actually going on around me. Still, I couldn't help imagining ahead to our arrival in Sioux City. We planned to take a day off the river there and go inland a bit and see our friends, John and Pat, in Spirit Lake. We knew them both well, though neither of us had seen them since they had married and had a child after graduating. John had been one of our roommates in college. We had shared a house together with several others and he, Jerry, and I were close. I imagined telling him and Pat about all we had seen and gone through. We would have the accomplishment of conquering the lakes and dams to brag about. They would be excited for us and impressed. My enthusiasm for the journey would revive. I might even phone Gloria and find her at home.

Paddle, I told myself, just shut-up and paddle.

In fact, there was nothing to do but keep on paddling—and, after all, every day brought the chance of something new, unanticipated. Around any bend, even on the lakes, we might run into an adventure. This thought kept me going as well.

It was about this time, July 15 to be exact, that something new did come along. We were nearing Mobridge. It was about five o'clock, and we were going to take a break and walk into town. We took some time out, however, to talk to two canoeists just setting out from a dock. He was a weatherman and quickly announced that all this recent rain was no fault of his. We laughed and as we exchanged stories with him he asked if we were doing any sailing.

Sailing?

He said he had outfitted a canoe he had in his garage with a ten-foot sail and it worked beautifully, depending, of course, on how strong the wind was.

In Mobridge at the Rainbow Café, Jerry and I sat eating one of their delicious, ninety-five cent chicken dinners and talked about sailing. We weren't going to buy any commercial canoe sail, even if there were such a thing. So how would we do it?

It took very little cogitating to solve the problem. We had two ponchos. One would be plenty big enough for a sail. It was easy to find two tree limbs and cut them to size, about seven feet long. We tied an arm of the poncho to each of the limbs, tied the bottom ends of the poncho in the same way, them wired one of the poles upright to the gunwale and left the other free. The following day the wind was up and, as luck would have it, blowing down river. We shoved off with me sitting in the bow seat, my feet braced against the two poles, which were upright and side-by-side. Once we were out a few hundred yards, Jerry yelled, "Okay, spread'em!"

I spread the poles so they formed a V, keeping my feet all the while braced against them where they met on the floor in the center of the bow. The wind bellied out the poncho-sail and the canoe jerked forward. We wobbled, listed heavily left, then right. I thought we were going over. I was about to lower the right side, untied pole and collapse the sail, but Jerry in the stern angled his paddle perfectly, using it as a rudder. We were sailing!

As I wrote in my journal, "What a gas to just sit back and roll on down the river. I could see ahead through the poncho's head opening. Jerry was pretty much at his ease back behind me. He is always talking about building or buying a sloop and this, I think, may be about as close as he'll come to it."

Figure 3.7 Sailing near Oahe Dam

The *Queen* may have looked a little strange out there on the wide waters of Oahe with this gray thing strapped up in front, but we were clipping along faster than we could have paddled.

The maiden voyage went well, but it was short. It was just too miserable a day. We were getting the old one-two punch from the wind and the rain. When the rain eased off, the wind took over and hit us with four-foot waves athwart the *Queen's* bow. We pulled into the bank and spent hours on the shore, eating berries, waiting, and as the wind died down, paddling on in the drizzle, then ducking back to shore for more berry picking. We sailed about six miles that first day before the ever-fickle wind did us in. After that, even with careful tacking, we couldn't make any speed. Finally, I took down the poles and laid them behind me.

So we did sail, here and on the lakes ahead, and, later, on the Mississippi. But the wind didn't cooperate often enough. Really, it became more an occasional diversion from catching water with the paddles than a way of making time. Still, a few days later we sailed all day, some seventy miles. Sailing was fun and, at the very least, a real energy saver. Unfortunately, as any veteran river traveler will tell you, the wind blows upstream nine times out of ten. Even when it blows downstream, it is unpredictable and erratic, especially in the rain. But since the sailing worked so well when it did work, we began to look around for other ways to get down the river a little faster. We had agreed in the beginning to avoid any sort of motor. Having a boat pull us, or having the *Queen* hauled any farther than it would take to get around a dam, was also taboo.

But on July 18, the day of our initiation as canoe sailors, we settled on another idea that might help us make more miles faster.

Jerry had been looking at the map since we hit lake Oahe for possible portage sites—not around dams but across peninsulas. At certain points on Oahe, we came to long hairpin bends in the river. We would paddle east for several miles, round a tip of land, paddle west the same distance, and end up with a narrow strip of higher ground covered with brush and trees, intervening between us and the bend where we started east. Our progress south, after all that work paddling, was almost nil. What if we could cut across the first leg of the hairpin journey and cross to the other side of the peninsula by means of a short portage, and then launch into the river again, saving time and reducing labor?

We scrutinized the bends as we came up on them and even got out to scout a few. The bend near West Whitlock was tempting. Still, the verdict was that portaging it would save almost no time and less labor. We decided to concentrate on those farther down river, closer to Pierre, North Dakota.

Shortly after we first sailed we made camp near a bend called Sully's Bend, not far from the little town of Agar. It is a dramatic neck of land, maybe ten miles long and at its widest point no more than two miles. This seemed like a perfect opportunity to try out our scheme for portaging.

There was impressive heat lightning all night on the eighteenth, but the day of the nineteenth dawned clear. We determined where the peninsula was narrowest and least marshy, and, rigging shoulder harnesses so we could carry all the gear across, started out. I took the bow since I was the taller of us.

It was slow going through willows, stands of sunflowers, and brush. We had to skirt patches of brambles and prickly pear cactus and forge on without benefit of a compass. Soon the view ahead was just like the one behind. Surrounded as we were by foliage, we could have been marching at the wrong angle, going parallel to the river. My own sense of direction is terrible. I hoped I could rely on Deacon to get us across to the river, despite the obvious exaggerations I had questioned a time or two in his stories of finding his way across the likes of the Red Desert and such near his home in Wyoming.

For thirty minutes we trudged along. I was beginning to have second and third thoughts about this whole portage-shortcut idea when abruptly we came out into a clearing and there was the river.

"Am I ye old faithful Pathfinder or what!" Jerry crowed.

I had to give him his due. He had directed us straight spot-on to a good launch site. We went back for the *Queen,* hoisted her up, and returned to our gear at a trot, or at least a very fast walk. That portage of less than an hour all told, saved us at least two and maybe three hours of paddling. Not to mention what an interesting experience it was.

The sun was out, there was no wind, and not even my chigger bites could spoil the triumph I felt as we paddled on toward the Oahe Dam.

By the afternoon of the next day, the twentieth, we were close to the dam, within fifteen miles. Our provisions were low; we had no rice or oatmeal. Breakfast was water based pancakes, no syrup. Several days running now, we had only blackberries for lunch and mac and cheese for dinner. As a result, for the first time on the trip, I was not feeling well. Stomach pain and diarrhea hit me during the nights and I woke feeling weak and discovered I had a severe case of hives. Never good at faking a bright, sunny disposition when I was miserable, I'm sure I was not the most pleasant traveling companion. Jerry, in his journal for this time writes, "Rich and I biting at each other . . ." And the next day: "Today we were civil in our exchanges for the most part."

This bickering would all change, I kept thinking, when we made the dam.

As we approached it that day an official looking pickup truck came toward us down a road that led to a large parking area. Two men wearing cowboy hats got out and stood hands on hips, watching us approach on the water. Then one waved us over to the shore. I wasn't sure what they meant to tell us, but I could see they were Corps of Engineers employees.

It turned out they were as close to a welcoming committee as we were ever to run into. They knew we were coming and not only helped us load the *Queen*, but hauled us and our gear around the dam, asking questions about our trip all the while. They even posed us for an official photograph. Evidently, our trip was being talked about along the river. This was long before cell phones, of course. What would it have been like had they had been available then? I'm sure the journey would have been better documented. Would it have added or detracted from our experience? I leave that judgment to your imagination.

Big Bend, Fort Randall, Gavins Point

Jerry's Journal, July 21

Portaged Oahe, heading for Big Bend. It's sunny and bright, a slow start; Rich sick. We stopped at Fort St. George near De Gray Island for water and ran into a Smithsonian crew excavating the old fort. We saw remains of half a dozen old foundations and several fireplaces, the charred floors of several buildings. Not many artifacts, evidently. Lee Madison was in charge—short and round with a sun hat and Hubert from Nebraska University at Lincoln—he showed us one stone pipe. There are many archeological crews in the area, he said, racing against time as Oahe backs up, especially concerned about excavating the remains of Arikara villages before they

go under forever. And also farther down stream, both Mandan and Arikara farming lands along the river bottom.

He said a good deal of the Crow Creek Reservation, which
surrounds Big Bend and Fort Thomson there, was already
submerged. Dakota and Lakota Sioux, chased off to Minnesota, then re-reservationed at Fort Thompson. We collected
our water at a farm and launched on down the river. Only
have about eighty miles of lake to paddle, Lake Sharpe. It was
slow going; we made only a few miles into the beginning of
the backwater from Big Bend Dam.

Big Bend Dam is located just south of the geographic feature it is
named for, a huge loop in the river, 25 miles long, with a "neck" less
than a mile wide. We considered trying to portage the narrowest part,
but looking at the map, I could see at a glance it wasn't practical because
of the terrain.

On the "front" or near side of this loop, as we headed east, the wind
blew hard in our faces. The water was choppy with occasional white caps
and this set the stage for one of the weirdest paddling incidents of the
trip. I dug up a fish, and a strange fish at that.

In his journal, Jerry describes what happened like this,

Head down, digging in against the wind and suddenly a
shovel nosed sturgeon landed in my lap. Seems Rich's paddle caught it on the back stroke and flipped it accidentally
around. Really caught me by surprise! Scared hell out of me.
It was 14 or 15 inches long—a scaly, armored, primitive, gar-
looking fish. Dropped him back in lake.

After settling down from the sturgeon in the lap trick, we rounded
the end of the loop and found the wind was now at our backs. So, we
raised our sail and made great time sailing east southeast down the far
side of the bend and into the dam.

The portage at the dam was an easy one; in fact, we paddled most
of it, since at that time the Big Bend Dam itself was not yet finished.
It would be a full year, well into the next July, before the embankment
we passed would be completed; it would be two more years before the

generators began humming. We were lucky, because today this earthen dam stands nearly a hundred feet high and is two miles in length.

When we were crossing it, there was very little backed-up river pushing against it. What we had experienced as slack water above the loop of the bend and around it was the backwater not of Big Bend, but of the next dam down the river, Fort Randall Dam. One could say that the reservoir behind Fort Randall Dam extended all the way up, or nearly so, to Oahe.

This meant that what little current there was in the river after Big Bend rapidly vanished. Once again we were paddling a lake, Lake Francis Case. I believed at the time the lake was named for a woman. This was unusual, I thought. How had it come to pass?

Sitting there in the bow of the *Queen*, paddling for hours on end, my mind often got caught up in such questions. Sakakawea had been a woman too, and had a reservoir named for her, but she was virtually a mythic figure. Sick during a lot of the Lewis and Clark journey, she came close to death. Pregnant, she gave birth to a child. And not long after that, acting as a mediator and interpreter for the group, she was responsible, in a very real way, for the success of the mission.

Perhaps Francis Case had been a sort of alter ego to Sakakawea? I imagined her as a white woman who had been abducted as a child by the Brule Indians and grew up to be a leader among them, proving herself as a brave warrior against the white invaders and later providing wise counsel when delegates from the Great White Father in the East appeared to negotiate treaties and, ultimately, removal of The People to an arid inhospitable reservation. I ruminated over other possible biographies for Francis Case, but it was this one I actually spend time writing down in my journal because I liked the way it goosed, so to speak, various clichés and stereotypes. It turned out, when years later I had a chance to look into who Francis Case actually was, I saw that I had the gender wrong. The spelling of the name would have been Frances if it were for a woman. Francis was a newspaperman and long time Republican politician, who won a name for himself fighting for improved infrastructure, mainly highways and rivers. An honorable, worthy man to be sure. Perhaps my version of whom the lake was named for derived from the tedium of my days paddling. I was young and bored and wanted a story with some romance and punch to it. Also, I was of the 60s. Like many another chauvinist and sexist male of my generation, I was aware and influenced, if only half consciously, by the various movements for social change during that era.

I didn't share my imaginings with Jerry. What was going on in his head, I won't venture to say. While I paddled, he called out that Lake Francis Case looked to be a little over a hundred miles long. He was studying the river map.

"It's the last of the big lakes on the Missouri," he said. "After we pass it, we get to Gavins Point Dam. The reservoir behind it, Lake Lewis and Clark, is only twenty-five miles long. Hell, we can do that in our sleep, right?"

He was right, but the tone of his voice told me what he was leaving unspoken. As I said, we were enduring mid-point blues, also known as halfway-there-let-down. I had felt it earlier than Jerry, but now we were both battling it. We had been out on the river fifty days and nights and we were worn down—not close to giving up, throwing in the towel, but definitely both threadbare of spirit and enthusiasm for the trip. We both knew there was a real question of whether, once we reached Sioux City and stopped at John's, we would be able to rally our energy enough to get back on the river right away.

At the moment, focusing on his question, I forced a hearty reply.

"Right on!"

Lewis and Clark would be a doddle, like crossing a pond. Then we would be into the free river again. There would be no more dams. No more dams all the way down to the confluence with the Mississippi and on to the Gulf.

Chamberlain, South Dakota, our next goal, was a small town of hardly more than 2000 inhabitants in 1962 and it is about the same today. It is the one town, however, that lies close to the river for many miles, which meant it was an important mail stop for us.

I had hoped we would make it at least by Monday, July 23. We were up at dawn that day and had Chamberlain in sight by noon. I was looking forward to picking up a letter from Gloria, getting a meal, and having a drink, something we hadn't done since Mandan, two weeks ago.

As we approached the town, however, we met with an unexpected problem. The river was higher than it had been for years, so high, it turned out, that there was very little daylight between the bridge, old US-16, and the river flowing beneath it. This may be hard to imagine if you look at that bridge today because it has gone through several permutations since 1962. Moreover, there are now two bridges crossing the Missouri at Chamberlain. The newcomer, down river from the US-16 Bridge, is the Interstate 90 bridge, built in 1972. In July of 1962, there was only one bridge and you couldn't fit a decent sized cottonwood tree trunk under it, let alone the canoe with us in it.

We paddled to the embankment near a bridge pier to scout out a way to do the portage. Jerry's journal has it that, ". . . so two cats helped us across the road and to the water." My journal has it that, we walked across the bridge, saw where we might possibly portage down the steep bank, then walked back across, considering the possibilities of letting the *Queen* drift down river and under the bridge on the end of a rope to be retrieved on the other side by one of us. A ridiculous idea.

So we stood there dejected about this added hurdle we faced with the town in sight when suddenly a passing car screeched to a halt just ahead on the shoulder and two men jumped out. A few minutes of palaver with Jerry and they fell to, helping us carry everything to an easy access point. My entry ended with, "Once again Fate, otherwise known as depending on the kindness of strangers, has stepped in to help us."

In Chamberlain we set up camp at the edge of the city park. Our cache of mail in General Delivery was larger than usual, with several letters each from Gloria and Betty and Jerry's folks. There was also a carefully wrapped package containing maps Jerry's dad, Raymond, had sent on. These were bound books from the U.S. Army Corps of Engineers, navigation charts mapping the Missouri River from above St. Louis to it confluence and the Mississippi River from the confluence to the Gulf. They were wonderful maps, showing not only the river and a mile on each side, but delineating the main channel, details of bridges, and all possible hazards, as well as posted mile markers. Also, if you were wondering how a small craft like ours would negotiate the locks at the confluence of the Missouri and Mississippi along side the huge barges, the Corps supplied full instructions.

We were reinvigorated, looking them over and drinking beer in a bar. Incredible! We had come at least halfway and only had a week's paddle or so to Sioux City, then less than 800 miles on to St. Louis. Cheering mail from our girlfriends, money from Jerry's parents, clean clothes, a good meal. Could heaven be any better?

Jerry's Journal, July 24

> Stayed in town late and got up late. The wind was blowing. A man named Cole stepped out of his trailer by the river and offered us a cup of java. Two young guys came along and offered Rich cigarettes. We all talked awhile. Finally, could not ignore the call from the river to get back on the water. Bucked the wind until we were around the point, then we set sail. We sailed the rest of the day with little paddling and much progress, about 50 miles. Camped by a huge deserted barn and house. The barn was broken down and caved in. The house had cow pellets in it; the cracks in the walls had flattened Union Leader tins nailed over them in even rows.
>
> We were up early the next day, number 51 of our voyage and the best breakfast yet of eggs, bacon, and spuds. Topped it off by picking ripe black berries for dessert.
>
> Jubilantly, we set sail for second day, a fair breeze carrying us past banks of choke cherries and junipers and even plum trees in the breaks. Camped about 15 miles above Fort Randall Dam.

At the Fort Randall Dam we once again found a Corps man to help make our portage. Our reception there was of interest and friendly. I have a vivid memory of one of the men who helped us. His name was Tobias and he said that Jerry and I were the first boat, canoe or otherwise, to cross the dam this year. That put a smile on both our faces; we felt "celebrated" in a small way. We were authentic river rats.

The Last Dam

Jerry spent a lot of time taking pictures, handing his camera over several times to someone else so he could take our picture. Soon we paddled on our way, talking about pushing hard, making Gavins Point the next day, Saturday, then getting into Sioux City by Monday.

I was feeling good by now. My paddle strokes were long and easy. The river was lazy, wide, and surrounded by greenery. I felt in tune with it, carefree.

The rain didn't set in again till late that evening. It rained from near midnight until 7:30 the next morning. Everything was soaked when we got up. There was more than an inch of water in the canoe. Jerry's camera got wet, meaning at least one roll of film was probably ruined. We knew the drill by now and without a word set about unloading the canoe and emptying out the water. We ate our breakfast of oranges, peanut butter and jelly sandwiches and milk, as we drifted down the river. It was 9:30 and we decided to see if by hitting it hard, we could make camp near the Niobrara River that night.

The Niobrara has its headwaters in Wyoming and runs through Nebraska to its confluence with the Missouri. Having looked at the map, I knew that we were still in South Dakota—if we paddled to the port side bank. But if we paddled starboard, we were in Nebraska. That amused me for a time as we paddled under skies that grew increasingly dark and threatening. Nothing but gloomy bottomland cornfields bordered the river. I kept reminding myself to "look again," to see what was unique to the countryside we were passing through. Occasionally, dense thickets of trees and brush edged the shore. Try as I might I could see nothing distinctive about them.

Yes, we were for sure and certain out of the West. The seclusion and solitude we had felt on the water all through Montana and most of North Dakota was gone. This was a much more public river. Whereas on the upper Missouri, we had rarely come across fishermen or other boaters, we saw them almost every day now. It was at first annoying. After all, this was *our* river. But we soon got used to happening on more river folk, and one good thing about it was that it made our regular searches for fresh drinking and cooking water a little easier. Most of the time we could depend on running into someone who would either direct us to clean water or simply allow us access to theirs. We would take the opportunity to socialize a little and get whatever information we could about the area. People who live on or near the river always enjoy talking about it and have plenty of stories to tell.

On this day, we had spotted a bright little spring, clear and clean looking, trickling over rocks, down into the river. My first thought today, in the present, would be that it was poisoned in some way, by some parasite, or bacterial pollutant. At the time, it didn't occur to me to even boil water as clear as this was. I'm sure I had giardia, or other such infections more than once on the voyage.

Having filled our bottles we set off. We were trying to reach the Niobrara River confluence and decided we would paddle down, pull the canoe in along a pier sporting several big boats and ask for information at one of the houses perched up on the bank and back from the river. As we approached, I saw we had entered a trailer park, a very up-scale one. I knew all about the silver Airstream trailers and doublewides, but I had never seen mobile homes like these. The one we stopped at was like a house, complete with porch, nice landscaping, awnings, and flower box-es. The young woman who answered our knocking spoke to us through the screen door. She was friendly enough though, and she listened with interest as Jerry explained what we were about. Evidently, we were only five miles from where the Niobrara came in. She told us what landmarks to look for. It was easy to miss because of the sandbars and because both rivers were high and water was flooding through the trees along the bank. We thanked her and turned to leave, but she stopped us. "Wait just a minute," she said.

When she came back, she pushed open the screen door and handed us a brown grocery bag. "That's eight eggs, two candy bars and some bacon." She grinned. "You two be sure and take care." And with that she closed the door.

Did I mention that she was a very good-looking woman, dressed like someone modeling what to wear for a resort holiday? As Jerry and I paddled away, elated at our good luck, we talked back and forth about her and what life must be like for these people summering on the river. I said they must be wealthy, but Jerry said no, people with real money and class didn't live in trailers, even big ones. We had paddled maybe two miles, before we heard a motor boat approaching from the rear. Hailing us, the pilot cut the engine, idling toward us and pushing waves our way so that the *Queen* rolled side to side a bit. I was prepared to be peeved, but the woman standing beside the man at the helm was the self same one we had just left at the un-mobile home. They introduced themselves as Jean and Gene Whittrock.

Jean, all smiles, asked if we might want to have dinner with them?

Do one-legged ducks swim in circles? We hadn't made any real distance that day—but some things were more important, at least in my mind, than keeping to the dictates of an arbitrary schedule: taking time out for a home cooked meal, for instance.

Beaching our canoe and pulling it up into the undergrowth so that it was pretty well hidden, we got aboard their boat with its big sixty horse-power Mercury engine and in no time we were sitting in their plush living room, talking river talk. Soon Jean had the dinner on the table: T-bone steaks, wonderfully delicious. She had laid out all the trimmings and seemed anxious to please us—and her husband, Gene. He let us know that he was a self-made man and proud of it. I can't bring back any details of our conversation, but I do remember he was generous with his beer supply and both of them had a few stories of their own to share about the Missouri and other rivers they had travelled far and wide. The four of us talked on into the evening and into the night. It was awkward to be leaving so late and Jean seemed on the verge of inviting us to stay the night, but Gene spoke up and said he would take us back to our boat. Jean hugged both of us as we left.

Using his boat's spotlight, Gene found where we had left the canoe. He let us off, waved, and roared away into the darkness.

It was a black night, moonless. We paddled out into it with some vague notion of having seen a clearing across the river earlier where we could camp. The surface of the river was dark and glimmering. There was no sound but that of our paddles and the distance insect choruses. There was also no way to tell where the sandbars were. Time and again we went aground. Then we made the channel. Then, nearing the opposite shore, we went aground again.

Both of us were grumbling as we put up the tent in the dark, blaming the other for not thinking to set up camp before going to the Whittrock's place. Jerry went silent, which meant that he was particularly irritated. I assumed he was angry, as was I, because we were off schedule, had over indulged, and stayed so late. I was saying something about getting up early, making up time and he cut me off short.

After a moment or two, I said, "At least it isn't raining."

But he was already asleep.

The next day, July 28, in a hurry because of yesterday's delay, we actually were up early. Paddling under gloomy skies a few miles down to a pier and ferryboat landing, we stopped for a late breakfast. I built a small fire and Jerry cooked up those lovely eggs and bacon that Jean had given us and the world brightened a little. For one thing the weather was clearing at last.

We were back in the canoe and on the river before noon, paddling at a slow but steady pace. By the time we camped we had made over forty miles. Therefore, we were covering about five miles an hour—not bad. We camped on a mud bar back from the water. We had made our goal of the previous day, the Niobrara River confluence, and many miles more. Now we were close to the dam. This fact heightened both our moods, and Jerry decided he would hike down river and scout out our landing site for tomorrow's portage.

This meant he would have to hike down a gully, then around the bluffs along the river, through dense brush, vine covered trees and massive greenery. It was rough going over to the powerhouse, I'm sure, and I had begun to worry a little as dusk came on. But he emerged out of the gloom to greet me cheerfully in his Brother Dave mode.

"Verily my good man. Found a great landing, easiest portage yet!"

He was mud up to his knees, scratched and disheveled, but all he could talk about was the fact that we would have no trouble crossing this, the last of the fifteen dams.

Gavins Point Dam to Sioux City

The next morning, fueled with more bacon and eggs, we headed out into the river where we soon ran into turbulent chop and swelling waves. Not one, but two, cruisers with their big outboards were roaring on down river. I hadn't realized this was such a busy access and egress point near the dam—but it was, especially now at the height of the summer season. We found ourselves paddling along among dozens of pontoon boats and various watercrafts.

Threading our way carefully to shore, we pulled into a boat dock near the dam. Just as Jerry had predicted, it didn't take long before we found someone from the Corps to help us across. As usual several of the men had questions to ask and gossip to share. One told us about a cruiser that was heading for South America and had been taken out of the water up at Fort Peck several weeks before and hauled down here to Gavins Point. A couple and their three children manned it. Launched with a bit of fanfare, it had cracked up below the dam near Yankton.

He seemed to relish the gory details and I asked him, in a round about way, if he were trying to spook us or warn us about some dangerous part of the river. He laughed and said he just thought it was part of his duty to remind us not to take the river for granted.

Indeed, it turned out that the river below the dam was a busy, hazardous place. We had to make our way carefully past the fishermen, the sandbars and the roaring boat traffic. I concentrated on my paddling, pushing aside my thoughts of that family on board the cruiser and their high hopes and misfortune. Yankton was only about eight miles away, and the boat wouldn't have been hard to spot, but we saw no sign of it. After docking near a Yankton marina, we walked in to mail letters and to buy a few supplies then went right back to our canoe.

Both of us were feeling a need to put this hectic section of water behind us.

Thankfully, before long the river began to narrow and the current picked up. Slowly it became its old self again.

Much later I learned that the Missouri immediately downstream of Gavins Point Dam has come to be valued for what it is, a national treasure. It is protected under the 1968 Wild and Scenic Rivers Act. This status came as part of the growing concern, especially during the 60s, about the environment and its depredation. Gaylord Nelson organized Earth Day in 1970, which was a matter of better late than never.

What was it like across the nation when Jerry and I were going down the river in 1962? The following quotation from the Earth Day website says it better than I could:

> At the time, Americans were slurping leaded gas through massive V8 sedans. Industry belched out smoke and sludge with little fear of legal consequences or bad press. Air pollution was commonly accepted as the smell of prosperity. "Environment" was a word that appeared more often in spelling bees than on the evening news.[15]

I remember often feeling a simmering resentment for the, "Dump it in the river and forget it" attitude as I paddled. This mentality was often evident along the banks, especially as we approached "civilization." Today, people are much more aware of how we have laid waste to our environment and its natural beauty. They are more sensitive to the fact that all life is interconnected. When the starfish die mysteriously by the thousands all the way down the West coast from Alaska to San Diego, as they are as I write this, we worry because no matter how remote their niche in the chain of life is from ours, if their ecological community changes fundamentally, ours will sooner or later be affected.

The Scenic Rivers Act did come a little late, but at least the section below Gavins Point and on to Sioux City hasn't changed much since we were there in '62. It is that rare bird, a stretch of the Lower Missouri that is even today free-flowing. That doesn't mean it is or was fast flowing or pristine. We found ourselves paddling between islands, easing past sandbars and snags, surrounded by miles-long stretches of marsh country. The mosquitoes, in keeping the immemorial traditions of their ancestors, did their best to eat us alive. But we knew this was the last of the non-channelized "natural" river we would see. It was with a good deal of ambivalence that we watched the trees and undergrowth disappear

---

15 http://www.earthday.org/earth-day-history-movement.

along the river banks, and morph into boats, docks, houses, and occasional factories. As we neared Sioux City, the shaggy and untamed river that we had been paddling died, in a sense, and the one replacing it was "civilized," dressed up with white banks of rock reinforcement, made presentable with wing-dikes and mile markers, maintained by dredges to a channel depth of nine feet.

I tried to stay focused on the fact that we had, "come through." According to the map, it was now only 740 miles of paddling to St. Louis. That meant we had knocked off a brutal and uncompromising 1700 miles of the Mighty Mo. Those miles were also incredibly beautiful, inspiring, and soul challenging. Still, we were now at least half way to our destination, New Orleans.

It was a time to celebrate and I was not looking back.

Sioux City and Old Friends

Sioux City was a ways off, actually. We had hoped to camp at Ponca State Park, which fronts the river, and paddle on into town the next morning. Finding the park proved difficult. It's name, Ponca, stayed with me for some reason, though, and years later I learned the story of the Ponca people and their Chief, Standing Bear.

The Poncas were removed to Indian Territory in 1877. A third of the tribe died either during or close on the heels of this move and many who survived were sick or disabled. When Standing Bear's sixteen-year-old son died, he decided the boy's remains would be buried at "home" so that his spirit would not wander the afterlife, lost forever. It took two months during the winter of 1879 for Standing Bear and a small group of Ponca's, mainly women and children, to travel back to the reservation of the Omaha where the burial ceremony was then performed near the place of his son's birth along the Niobrara River.

Of course, for the Poncas to leave the reservation in Oklahoma was illegal and they were arrested under order of the Secretary of the Interior as a renegade band. To his everlasting credit General George Crook was moved by Standing Bear's plight, enlisting the aid of Thomas H. Tibbles, an Omaha newspaperman, who hired top-notch lawyers. In Standing Bear v. Crook , the Government pursued its case on the grounds that Native Americans were not "persons under the law." Standing Bear's lawyers fought the case under the aegis of the fourteenth Amendment to the Constitution, which had become law only ten years before, following the Civil War, and was to figure importantly in such cases as Brown v. The Board of Education. Standing Bear won his case. It was an important victory, a milestone in the struggle by Native Americans and also African Americans to gain recognition under the law as human beings, protected under the Constitution and with full rights appertaining thereto, including the right to vote.

As I read this, I recalled how Lewis and Clark had addressed the Indians as "Children." It seems to me that as Jerry and I journeyed south and east down the rivers, we also journeyed ahead in time through decades of a human rights struggle that continues to this moment.

I am left to wonder if this would have occurred to me at the time, had we found Ponca Park and read the historical information afforded there. As it was, we spent the day navigating through the sandbars and islands and were never sure where the park began or left off.

Finally, we saw a man on the bank and called out to him for directions. This was Chuck Bellman, who was, as it turned out, the publisher of the *Vermillion Plain Talk* newspaper. He was doing a feature on the river and snapped a few shots of us. Having taken our mailing address, he promised to send on copies. This was the first time we had been noticed by the media, as we call it now. Neither of us made much of it and figured if he published the photos and sent them on to us, fine. If not, that was fine too. It had begun to drizzle again and we needed to set up camp somewhere.

Figure 3.8 Towboat near Sioux City

July 30 we were up early. For breakfast it was rice and powered milk, made palatable with a heavy sprinkling of cinnamon. As we ate, I noticed the wind had come up and it was blowing down river for a change. We did a rapid clean and stow, then got onto the water.

The wind wasn't strong; the sail had to be tended carefully to get the right tack, but, nonetheless, this was better than paddling and I had a little more time to look around. Levees lined both sides of the river. Barges nosed in along the levees, working on them, unloading rock for the most part. The country was flat bottomland, with hills against the far horizon. The banks were festooned now with boats and houses and soon we heard the roar of traffic: Sioux City, Iowa.

Finding a place to dock wasn't as easy as we had anticipated. We wanted to pull in at a marina, track down a telephone, and call John, our friend up in Spirit Lake. It was only a little over a hundred miles from there to where we were. If he drove down to pick us up after work, fine, but hopefully he would be able to get the afternoon off. We saw a barge loading operation ahead and pulled into shore nearby, tying up to a post jutting out of the rocky embankment.

While Jerry went off to find the foreman, or whoever might have authority enough to let us leave our canoe in the company's dock area, I looked for a phone booth. Spotting one at the edge of a parking lot. John, it turned out was at home. It was great to hear his voice again. He sounded surprised and delighted to hear mine. I told him where we had docked and we talked for a few minutes then he paused. He said he had been hoping we would be in on a weekend. Today was Monday. There was a little upset at home, he said; he would explain later.

"Never mind, nothing to worry about. I'll take off and find you guys—even if I have to drive the length of the river. Just be on the look-out for a new black Plymouth. No problem."

I hung the phone up and walked away from the booth frowning. No problem? Why wasn't he at work? He hadn't mentioned his infant son or Pat, brushing aside my question about her with a quick. "Oh, she's okay. She hanging in."

Good old John. He had been a drama major; maybe that explained something, but this wasn't exactly the welcome I had been hoping for. Meeting Jerry back where we had docked, I told him my news, leaving out my uneasiness. He in turn said the foreman had given us permission to tie up near one of the barges that was being repaired, back out of the way of their work.

"Hey," he said, "something else. This guy had sort of been expecting us. Weird, there was a woman from a newspaper who stopped at this place and the marina farther up, asking about us. Evidently she wants to do a story on us. How about that?"

I supposed that this was in some way Chuck Bellman's doing and didn't give it much thought. Jerry called the number he had been given by the foreman and spoke to a Gail Stilwell of the *Sioux City Journal*. She said she would be right down—in an hour. We should wait—right where we were.

We agreed, but we had our own chores to deal with. First there was the matter of finding the post office and collecting our mail, and then a celebratory beer and meal somewhere.

We might have been gone more than an hour, but in any case she drove up just as we got back to the canoe. Her car, a noisy Ford, had seen better days, but she was a trim, pretty woman with dark short hair, jeans and white sweater. Greeting us both by name, she started off by asking about the spelling of the name of the canoe—wasn't it unusual? It was, we agreed, and let it go at that. We answered her questions regarding who we were, where we'd come from, what we'd seen, and where we were going straightforwardly enough. Our earlier meeting with Mr. Bellman had prepared us a little for this sort of rapid-fire interrogation. She wanted more details though, some "human interest" material.

I felt she was encouraging us to ham it up a little, embellish a few incidents here and there. But then neither of us needed much encouragement to do that. I found myself enjoying the interview. Jerry, with his gift of gab obviously felt the same way. Basking in her wide-eyed attention to our every word, we must have increased our hat size considerably.

An hour later, Gail Stilwell roared off, having snapped a dozen photos of us standing like intrepid adventurers, or so we fancied, with the *Queen* and the river in the background.

Then began the waiting for John. Around seven we heard a car horn honking incessantly and went up to the road to see that he had arrived and no mistake about it. He got out; we all took turns clapping each other on the back. He was laughing, shaking his head. "No luggage," he said, "no bags. Bums. You guys are amazing, just amazing."

And we were off to Spirit Lake. He had a couple of six packs in the car (no open container law in those days) and I am sure we regaled him with tales of our encounters all along the river. It wasn't until we had gotten to his home, been greeted by Pat, whom we knew well from our college days, and been invited to sit down in the kitchen for something to eat and drink, that I learned about their trouble.

They were worried sick over their year old son, who was in the hospital, due for minor surgery in the morning. We were all good friends and I listened sympathetically. No surgery is minor, especially for an infant; you didn't have to be a parent to understand what they were going through. We traded news about mutual friends; John told us about his job as a manager at a small factory nearby and how much he hated it. It dawned on me that crowing about our footloose exploits was not going to make them feel any better. Jerry could make anybody laugh, even two anxiety distracted parents and for a brief time it seemed like the old days of two years ago, but the night ended early. Pat excused herself to get things ready for the visit to the hospital in the morning and not long after John showed us to the extra bedroom where we would be sleeping.

The next morning the two of them were already gone by the time Jerry and I managed to rouse ourselves. Cereal and milk and fruit were on the table. By the time we had indulged ourselves with the luxury of long hot showers, a slow breakfast and several cups of coffee, John was back. The surgery had gone well, the baby was out of any danger. Pat was staying with him. Energized and upbeat, he kept repeating that we had to stay another night. He wanted to show us around town, show us where he worked, we'd go to Milford. He had been looking forward to seeing us, and hearing about our trip; we had to stay.

So we stayed. We stopped briefly by his office to look around, then went to an amusement park. He bought us beers in Milford, nearby, and through the afternoon the three of us exchanged stories and memories. I had read that a group of Spirit Lake's early settlers were killed in a Sioux raid; he hadn't heard anything about it. More than anything else, he talked about his job. He seemed to be brooding over the mentality of the people he worked with and what he called "the system." I figured his mood grew pretty directly out of his concern for his child. He was doing his best to entertain us, but this just wasn't a day for the big reunion we had all talked about.

We left the next morning. Clearly, John had to stay close to home so Jerry and I decided to hitch-hike back to the river. John, apologetic, drove us to edge of town and dropped us off. As he drove away, two women going to a chiropractor appointment in Sibley stopped for us. The driver's first question was, "Are you the river boys?" To which Jerry responded with his standard, cheerful reply, "You ain't wrong!" They dropped us off an hour later and we quickly got another ride on into Sioux City, arriving before noon.

By 2:30 we were headed down the river again, glad to be back on the water, intent on reaching our next mail stop—Decatur, Nebraska. I thought of John and Pat. We had last seen them in the heady days of graduation parties and grand plans. Now here they were two years later, struggling with a situation none of us could have imagined at that time.

As I paddled mile after mile, alternating my position between sitting and kneeling on my life preserver as a cushion, did I take anything to heart from their situation and apply it to my own impending marriage to Gloria? I had tried to call her three or four times but was told she was out. Out where? Whoever answered had no idea. Still, as far as I can tell from my journal entries, I shrugged this off. Thinking of John and Pat's situation, I didn't feel it could apply in any way to us or our plans. And though I felt bad for them and hoped their baby would be all right, I'm sure I soon became absorbed again in the rhythms of paddling and watching the tree lined river bank for signs of animal life. Ah, youth.

We were traveling that section of the river now known as the Lower Missouri, passing through rich farming country with dense foliage and cornfields looming like green walls on either side of the river. Buoys marked the channel, courtesy of the Corps of Engineers, and the channel current swung along at a good clip, three to four miles an hour. We'd spot a white mile marker sign with its black numbers from time to time. Levees and dikes lined the banks. Occasionally, we passed sand dredges or a noisy pile driver hard at work.

The dredges caught my attention. They were sometimes moored by a line out in the middle of the channel: you didn't want to come around a tight bend and find yourself heading smack on for one, then avoid it only to clip its mooring cable. Moored barges could be a problem too, if you got too close. The wide front end of a barge is undercut, that is, raked, so if a boat like ours is caught against the front of the barge, the current can suck it right under.

And there were the towboats, which were 30 to 200 feet long, generally 20 to 50 feet wide with tall, padded steel uprights in front used to push strings of barges, as many as fifteen, four or five abreast on the Missouri above St. Louis, and up to forty on the Mississippi. These boats and their rectangular lattice of barges, called "rafts," chugged past us both day and night, churning up four-foot swells. The towboat rafts we first met on the Missouri were relatively short and increased in length as we approached the Mississippi, where some of them were truly huge. In the beginning they were easy to avoid and the waves they created provided us with a little diversion. We would pivot broad side to the current and steer the *Queen* into the huge swells so we could ride them. One deck hand on a barge yelled at us repeatedly and finally, over the noise of the engine, I made out what he was saying: "You people must be CRAZY!"

He had a point. For instance, somehow we had pushed off from Sioux City without drinking water. We had to stop by a place not far from the river and ask if we could fill our jugs. There were ducks in the yard and the man of the house told us to take what we wanted from the pond nearby. A woman with no teeth, his wife I presumed, came out on the porch at this juncture and scolded him, saying, "You know that water ain't fit to drink!" Turning to us, she said, "You boys just go on back of the house and help yourselves from the hand pump." This we did. The water was brown with rust no matter how much I plied the handle, but we thanked her kindly and went our way. In camp we boiled the water. The color did not change and neither did the acrid iron taste.

The next day, Thursday, August 2, we stopped for a short time on the west side of the river, the Nebraska side, and walked into Decatur, mile marker 691, where we met a man who laughed at our brown water story and gave us both a soda pop. Then he filled our jugs with city water, which we assumed, of course, was absolutely pure—and who wouldn't prefer the taste of chlorine to iron?

Two days later we pulled into the River Club Marina, mile marker 619, near Omaha and docked. We had made the seventy or so miles from Decatur without pushing hard. It had been two days of wind in our faces, but no rain. Omaha was the biggest conglomeration of factories, industrial plants, corporations, vehicles, streets, highways, buildings, and houses, not to mention people, that we had come across in our journey thus far. It made Great Falls or Sioux City look like villages. Jerry knew a friend of the family who lived here, George Erpelding, and phoned him. He picked us up and showed us around town. At his place we cleaned up, then all of us went out to Little Frank's, and I, for the first time in my life, had a filet mignon. I marveled at how small it was—but four inches thick, tender, juicy and delicious!

At John and Pat's place, I had appreciated the amenities of civilization: a hot shower, shampoo, a mattress you didn't have to inflate via lung power, but here in what to me was a luxurious apartment, they seemed more precious. Bright lights, big city, good conversation—and people, scads of them all over. Just to walk the streets and people-watch was entertainment enough. But George actually had a television set. Commercial television broadcasting had been around, even in the mountains of Colorado, before the fifties. In Glenwood Springs my uncle had bought my Grandmother a big console, which picked up a few channels, but always in snowy black and white. George's television received color programming and it was clear. Incredible!

Nonetheless, I woke the next day ready to be back on the water. After shopping for supplies, including a good mosquito bar, much needed, we pushed off, heading for Plattsmouth. Before we left, as we were chatting with the marina owner, he told us we were the second long-haul canoe to come through that summer. Nine days before, two lads coming down the river from Bismarck had stopped over for a while. Neither of us thought much about this, since the two, so we were told, were only going down as far as St. Louis.

We camped near the Plattsmouth Boat Club dock and before we could get a fire going, a correspondent from radio station WOW showed up to interview us and take a few pictures. I was beginning to get annoyed by now at some of the questions that kept coming up, particularly any having to do with the idea that we were doing a backward Lewis and Clark trip. It was a catchy phrase but annoyingly inexact. Just as the WOW interviewer left another man came toward us from the marina office. He introduced himself as M.J. Hill, representing the *Plattsmouth Semi-weekly Journal*.

Marshall Hill proved himself right off the bat by offering to leave us in peace for the evening and come back in the morning around eight. Hungry and tired, we agreed. Eight o'clock came mighty early, however.

Jerry and I managed to stumble out of the tent and there was Marshall—with coffee. We answered his questions and posed for a few photos, which he later sent on to Jerry's mom and to Gloria with a letter explaining how he had met us and that we, ". . . both looked good and were in the best of spirits." Like I said, he was a good man.

We paddled off, waved back at him, and made our way down past Nebraska City by noon. Floating for a while, we ate lunch on the water and then paddled hard down to just below Brownville. Both these towns were typical river towns, established around 1850, booming for a few decades as commercial centers served by the steamboats, then dwindling as the railroads rendered steamboats superfluous. Close to the slave-holding state of Missouri, both were important stops on the Underground Railroad during the Civil War. We took a walk around Brownville, but other than its history it had little to offer.

We seemed to have outlasted the rains, though the weather was hot and humid. The river banks, lined with scrub trees, broken by the occasional bluff, didn't offer much of interest to the eye. As Jerry remarks in his journal, "The river's beginning to look like a huge irrigation ditch." Still the activity on the river had picked up considerably and caught our attention. Though motorboats or launches passed once in a while, they never were close enough to worry about. Tugboats and their barges dominated the river traffic and took some getting used to. We learned to identify the engine noise of an approaching tug, whether it was coming up from fore or aft, and ultimately were even able to judge fairly well from the volume and tenor of the laboring engine how big a raft it was pushing our way.

At Weeping Water, another small town with docks and boats, sporting a park beside the river, there was a steam dredge operating down the channel and a little farther on, a pile driver reinforcing a levee. They were examples of the Corps' constant efforts to maintain the channel and to engineer the course of the river. It was interesting to watch the work and we paused here a long time.

Figure 3.9 Dredge, The William M Black

Jerry took the above photo (Figure 3.9) when we were down on the Mississippi, but I include it here to give an idea of what these steam dredges were like. The *William M Black*, pictured above was one of the last and best of the paddle steamers on the river. A side-wheel steam paddle dredge with a length of 268 feet, housing a standard operating crew of 49, it could dredge 80,000 cubic yards of silt a day. It was a dustpan dredge, which means it used water jets and suction to dig. Unfortunately, it also used 7000 gallons of heavy oil a day to operate. Decommissioned in 1972, it is now a floating museum, part of the National Mississippi River Museum and Aquarium.

By Monday, August 6, we were in Rulo, which sits on a slight rise above the river where the borders of Kansas, Nebraska and Missouri converge. The sky was clear, the sun bright. Paddling out on the river was hot, thirsty work, and we went into town to have a cold beer. We sampled several bars in Rulo, each dimmer and more depressing than the last. The town had a checkered past, according to a man we spoke to in a place called Loopers. He was evasive, hinting at several scandals, but nothing he said seemed interesting enough to follow up. Looking out the window, I saw blind storefronts and vacant streets. A pall hung over the entire area.

When we got back to the canoe, thinking that the town's name seemed familiar, I checked the Corps navigation maps. Sure enough the very first chart was titled from the source, that is St. Louis, to Rulo. The distance covered was 497.5 miles. On a good day we were making about 60 to 75 miles. That meant we were only a little over a week away from the Mississippi River and St. Louie.

Somehow this made the possibility of actually finishing up this long first leg of the journey seem much more within our grasp, which in turn reminded me that I had a clutch of relatives living not even an hour's drive from St Louis. What better time to contact them and see if we couldn't all do some celebrating?

As we went on down the river, we were coming across towns I had either driven through or seen many times on road maps. The day after Rulo we stopped at the Yacht Club Marina at Atchison; the next day we had an early lunch break in Leavenworth. It was a special day for me as I noted in my journal: "August 8, Gloria's birthday: hoping you were "born" this day into happiness, my love." As I wrote this, we were sitting at a table in a tavern near the river. I looked up and a man sat down opposite us and introduced himself as Shorty. He was a Deputy Sheriff. He had seen us walk up from the river and was curious about us. But not in a professional way, he said. We proceeded to get into a drawn out conversation with him about the river towns and Leavenworth in particular. When Jerry remarked on the shells of old buildings we had seen and the "For Sale" signs that abounded, he launched into a long spiel defending the city. Did we know anything about how important Leavenworth was historically?

"You mean for its prison?" I asked.

"Oh, no, Sir," he said. "Let me tell you, there's plenty more."

We weren't about to stop him and for the next hour he regaled us with anecdotes about the Planters Hotel. Evidently this hotel figured prominently in the struggle between Abolitionists and Pro-slavery groups in town. The Planters hotel figured in most of them. Lincoln had slept there. He had stood on the steps in front of the hotel and admonished the crowd to settle the slavery question at the ballot box. During the Civil War, the Planters was a stop on the Underground Railroad. A barber at the Planters was a runaway slave and when he was recognized as such and detained, Abolitionists stole him away from his captors. He was never caught.

After a time it was became clear that his sympathies weren't with the Abolitionists. Finally, I said, "And these days?"

That was enough to draw him up short. He lapsed into silence and beckoned for another round. Jerry and I exchanged looks. It was a matter of honor not to turn down a free beer, but we told him we had to be on our way.

Figure 3.10 Kansas City

Paddling on downriver and passing under several huge bridges with an impressive skyline on both sides, we found ourselves in heavy barge traffic. Kansas City, Kansas loomed on one side of the river and Kansas City, Missouri on the other. Docking at the Sharlynn Marina, we asked about camping nearby and if we could fill our water jugs. Jerry and one of the owners, Dick Lynn began talking about Wyoming. Soon it seemed like we had all known each other for ages. We were given free use of the marina's facilities, which meant a hot shower, clean clothes, and food.

I lay on my sleeping bag happy that night. In my head I was writing Gloria a letter, as I often did before falling asleep. Her last letter had been filled with details of preparations for our wedding, who had come to her "shower,' what gifts she/we had received.

And where was she right now, what was she doing? All I knew was that her birthday hadn't turned out so bad after all—for me. And I hoped the same were true for her.

The next morning, we rolled out by seven. Dick had said he would take us on a Cook's tour before we left so after breakfast we got into his VW van and rode into the city. After sightseeing, we had lunch at Johnny's Chili Place. By two o'clock we were back on the water. Pulling into the Sharlynn had definitely turned out to be a very lucky break for us.

Of course, luck is nothing if not fickle and by three o'clock it was raining hard and the thunder was rolling down the river. We paddled on and made 32 miles before we camped across from Napoleon, Missouri. The town of Wellington lies just a few miles up river and in between we had come past a sign for Waterloo. Evidently, the local city founders had a sense of humor or no imagination at all.

Up early again the next day, we fueled ourselves with pancakes and paddled until around noon when we came to Lexington, Missouri. There we saw a silver Alumacraft canoe snugged up bow and stern against the embankment near the local park. Farther back beneath a tree, stood a blue nylon tent. Generally, we would have passed on by to find our own spot, but we needed water so we paddled shoreward.

This turned out to be a momentous decision.

Multiplying and Dividing

Figure 3.11
Jerry, Rich and Harold Umber; photo by Bill Shirley

Paddling in and docking, we grabbed our water jugs and walked up the embankment past the blue tent, which was pitched near a picnic table. Inside the tent were two sleeping bags. On top of the bags I could make out two sprawled, shadowy forms.

Jerry and I continued past, and, cutting through a cornfield, walked into town. Returning, we stepped out of the corn stalks and surprised the two canoeists just as they were getting out of their tent. Despite being startled at the sudden appearance of two river rats who were even shaggier then they were, they greeted us with grins and it wasn't long before the four of us were trading stories.

They were, indeed, the two canoeists from Bismarck whom we had heard about. They had been nine days ahead of us, but evidently they were in no hurry. Introductions went back and forth. The taller, dark haired one was Harold Umber, the shorter, light haired one was Bill

Shirley. When Jerry took out his pipe and lit it, Bill and Harold followed suit. As the four of us sat around the picnic table smoking our pipes, it soon became evident that we were pretty simpatico.

With the afternoon advancing, the heat of the day began to bear down and someone said something about going into the town. Securing our gear as well as we could, we started off. Lexington was close by, up on the bluffs. Harold told us he and Bill had checked things out here the day before. There was actually a cannon ball lodged in a column of the courthouse, a remnant of the Civil War battle of Lexington. The only other cool thing about the place, according to Bill, was that there had been a steamboat explosion here in the 1850s that killed 150 people.

Figure 3.12 Bill and Harold

We laughed, not because these events were funny, it just seemed ironic to Jerry and me because we had had several conversations recently about how all the river towns sported plaques and brochures that let folks know certain tidbits of violence and mayhem that made them famous.

We found a friendly looking tavern and stepped inside. Several slow-turning ceiling fans cooled the interior. The server, a burly, bearded man, met us with a smile. Just our kind of place. One round led to another and the afternoon gradually shifted over into evening mode. We had dinner, then went back along the dimly lit streets and down to the park and the canoes. All was as we had left it.

I went to sleep that night thinking that it was good to talk about the river with fellow voyageurs who knew exactly what we meant.

By noon the next day we had all decided to travel together. Bill and Harold, who had set out with St. Louis as their goal, decided to go on down with us to New Orleans and the Gulf.

Lexington to St. Louis

My river journey with Jerry ended at Lexington, Missouri. That is, our journey to New Orleans that he and I began together at Three Forks, Montana, June 4, ended on August 10, after around 2000 miles in tandem. There were four of us now. Four of us, paddling, going ashore, sharing meals, developing a new four-way friendship. The 24-7 experience of traveling alone with another person, sitting in a canoe with him all day, sharing everything together, was over for us.

That, I suppose, was good, mostly. After all, to live constantly in such proximity to anyone, even your best friend, is a strain on both parties. Jerry could get to be pretty crotchety. Often times, if I wasn't irritable, I was zoned out, lost in my own thoughts. We kept getting confused about who was Huck and who was Jim.

Still, when it came right down to it, even after Lexington, we spent most of our time with each other. Bill and Harold, in their shorter canoe, couldn't keep up with the *Queen*. She was lighter than their craft and not as wide in the beam. Unlike their canoe, she had a keel, which meant that for us navigation, or forward progress, was a little surer on the open river, particularly in the wind, and hence we were faster.

The big changes came when we were off the water, in camp, making our meals, sharing them, or going into towns along the way as a fearsome foursome.

Also, the trip had taken on a new character because the river we were paddling now had changed so drastically. More and more it was totally tamed. The channel was clearly marked. There were bare patches of revetment along the banks, riprap, and more jetties, pilings, and levees. All this engineering to control the river was deemed necessary because in the old days it had run amuck every spring. Its floods created a tragic loss of life. The property damage involved was staggering. But beginning with the Flood Control act of 1917, plans were set in motion to build dams and to transform the river, so its flooding would be controlled.

Achieving this latter goal was largely a matter of building up the banks with levees and "channelizing" the river. In its natural state the Mighty Mo's spring run-off created flood plains miles wide. When the river gradually withdrew in mid-summer to its original winding course, new bends, or meanders, were formed as the moving water eroded sediments from the outside of a bend and deposited them farther down on the inside. By 1962 this was no longer so. Extending dikes out into the river at strategic points on both sides and constant dredging had brought a halt to this age-old process. Silt was deposited behind the dikes, creating new bottomland, and the river was gradually wedged into shape, so to speak, and forced to toe the line. Through its program of continuous dredging, the Corps of Engineers was able to establish and maintain a constant channel, nine feet deep from the Gulf to Sioux City.

So the river was not as wild or interesting as it had been in its natural state. Nonetheless, the views from where we sat on the river were often beautiful. There were still towering bluffs. The shoreline with its ragged stands of trees, broken by fields of corn, and featuring docks, motor boats, and small houses, was constantly changing. There was still wild life, birds flitting from tree to tree down the river ahead of us, terns or plovers on the sandspits. Occasionally a sharp-shinned or red-tail hawk swooped down just above the water. The arid scrubland, the huge old cottonwoods, the thick stands of lodge pole pine, spruce and fir were gone. But the trees we saw now, the eastern cottonwood, sprawling willow, box elder, and ash were beautiful too, especially in the evening with the golden light of the sun playing off their leaves. It wasn't unusual to catch sight of a white tail deer, and along the banks we occasionally saw raccoon, opossum, and muskrat, and at least once, a fox.

Actually, during this stretch to St. Louis the towns along the way, rather than the scenery, came to dominate our experience of the river. Most of the towns were small like Waverly, Miami, Glasgow, and Arrow Rock. Towns that, like Nebraska City, had been nurtured by the river's steamboat trade. Towns that began to die when the railroads came and diverted commerce farther to the west. In 1962 the barge traffic was still thriving, but many of the towns we saw along the river were drying up. When we walked into Waverly, once a commercial center for a large area, what we saw were mainly faded signs and boarded up stores in empty buildings. Waverly had suffered a diminishment not unlike that which many towns along the interstate highway routes were to suffer decades later as they were bypassed.

This, somewhat perversely, made the towns more interesting to us. Without really deciding to, we became "urban explorers." The river was our natural habitat and the towns were the wilds we would hike into for adventure.

For instance, on August 13 we pulled into Booneville. Booneville had faded from its glory days but still had vitality. Walking into town, we first hunted down a place to find fresh water, then we looked for somewhere to buy a drink or two. We would buy supplies and fill our jugs on the way back to the river. Jerry and I had gotten into the habit earlier of asking old timers in the taverns we visited about their town and had always found they needed very little prompting. In Booneville we got a little more information than we bargained for.

I had surmised that Booneville was named for Daniel Boone, but quickly learned that, "No, sir, it was named for his two sons." There was a town in Tennessee name for Daniel though, Boonsboro, and, in fact, all you had to do was consult state maps to see the Boones were very influential folk in Missouri. A man with a soft Texas drawl sitting at the end of the bar was not happy with the notion that Daniel Boone was, "such a big deal."

"What about Davy Crockett?" he asked. "Y'all ever hear of him? Why he's got more towns in Tennessee and Texas named after him than Carter got little liver pills."

Soon a discussion began about who was the greatest hero: Daniel Boone or Davy Crockett.

Daniel had killed a "bar" with his bare hands, but Davy had died in the battle of the Alamo and was found surrounded by ten dead bodies of Mexican soldiers and his knife sticking in the chest of one who had fallen across him. The debate grew heated. It ended only when it was declared a deadlock tie by the barkeep. He sealed his declaration by serving up a round of free beer.

Later, in Jefferson City, named, of course, after that illustrious sponsor of the Lewis and Clark expedition, and one of the few American cities actually built to be a state capitol, we noted, once again, that people on the street were stopping to gawk at us. We were heading downtown toward the state capitol museum, having just come out of the Nite of the Nite tavern where the server had "Born to Lose" tattooed on her arm. As we stood waiting for the light to change at a corner, we saw a woman across the street taking a photo of us. Jerry quickly swung up his camera and took a few shots of her in return. This developed into what Jerry called, "candid snaps of unwary urbanites," wherein we would split up and stand on opposites corners with both Jerry and Bill taking pictures across the street of people's reactions as they saw us. Beat up hats, uncut hair, sunburned faces, beards, and wearing shorts or dingy pants, we were an unusual sight. People stared, some averted their eyes and others grinned and kept walking. No one spoke directly to us, though we overheard some mumbling. Wide spread homelessness and pan-handling in the cities was in those days minimal. We didn't quite fit into the Beatnik stereotype and we didn't have motorcycles. We looked like bums, but we didn't act like bums.

If Jerry and I had been alone, we wouldn't have been quite so obvious about putting on the public. Still, we all had a lot of laughs doing this and more. Today, of course, the cell phone shots would have gone out instantly. Or, more likely, we would be totally ignored.

Jerry's Journal, August 15-16

Left Jeff City about 1:30. We made a big push to Washington. There are fewer bluffs now and more hills. We passed a U.S. Coast Guard shipyard at Gasconade and talked to an unlucky fisherman who was jugging.[16] Stopped briefly at Herman. Paddled on and made Washington near 5:40; Rich went into town for the mail. Bill and Harold were about ten minutes behind us. Folks sent a little transistor radio for us. Three letters went back. I'm missing Betty. Washed clothes and got a ride from the slightly paranoid owner of the place. Talked to barkeep in the Old Dutch Tavern. Nice guy. He gave us all corncob pipes. Stopped by the Sammy Davis Bar later— owner showed me his pocket Colt. He had a son-in-law who worked for Morse Implement in Denver.

Thursday. Up early, hot already at 8 o'clock. Went to the Railroad Hotel for breakfast. Checked for mail again and then arranged for a tour of the corncob pipe factory at 2:00. Met Bob Mahon at the post office. He invited us for a case of beer tonight. I called home for money and we had to wait to pick it up until 3 o'clock, after our tour of the pipe factory, which was a gas. Bought some groceries. Mahon picked us up at six and we went to his home to eat pork steaks. We talked of philosophy and small town people. He had a fiberglass canoe, a Herters, bad. His son was a writer and had won 2nd in a short story contest. We stayed till midnight. I asked if I could use his phone. I called Betty. Couldn't sleep for the heat.

Rich's Journal, August 15-17

We pushed hard into Washington yesterday, made 58 miles, but missed our five o'clock deadline by 30 minutes. I walked up to the post office anyway and inside rapped on the closed window.

---

16 A method of "fishing" whereby plastic jugs are strung together out into the river with lines and baited hooks attached, anchored, and then checked on periodically.

After a little commotion, I succeeded in getting the mail. However, it was a disappointing letter from Glo and it still gnaws at me.

We terrorized a laundromat without really trying for an hour, then had a drink and went back to camp by the river. The next mail stop will be St. Genevieve, MO, then Cairo, IL, both below St. Louis on the Mississippi!

Today, August 17, we were in St. Charles. The river has become more and more straitjacketed, pilings and dikes and green banks, a few interesting bluffs. We are riding wide, muddy water that began as pure snowmelt at 14,000 feet about two thousand miles west of here up on the Continental Divide. Jerry finally got the mosquito bar working right, earning my eternal gratitude, and all of us built a huge camp fire, then popped some corn over the embers. Jerry, Bill, and Harold stayed up talking hunting, guns, cars, and racing. I went to bed. This is a beautiful morning. I am excited to be heading for the Chain of Rocks canal and my first paddle on the Mississippi. Will call Uncle Roy, maybe all of us hitchhike up to see Uncle Ernest, Aunt Louise, Aunt Leona, Mr. Nagel, Uncle Ray, Aunt Norma, and Uncle Elmer—the lot!

I liked St. Charles, an interesting little town with a river front street that had managed to preserve its older buildings. This was before the tourist industry began to realize the money to be made from developing Historical Districts and putting up bronzed commemorative plaques everywhere. I went into town alone and stopped to look over the old houses. There was a tavern on the corner not far from the post office, and as I went in I was surprised to see children playing near the tables with their parents looking on, smiling over steins of beer. I realize now, looking back, that this establishment was modeled on a German Gasthaus, a kind of bar and restaurant in Germany that functions as a social center for a neighborhood. I talked to an old man at the bar and he told me many of the people in and around St. Charles were of German immigrant ancestry, which was interesting to me since my mother's people, whom I hoped to see soon, were only a generation removed from Germany. My grandmother and my mother would talk to each other in German at times, especially when my brother and I weren't meant to understand what they were saying, but there were no stories bandied about of the old country. Nor was the language passed on to the younger generations, my brother, sister, and me, or our cousins. I'm sure the First World War put a dent in the popularity of all things German and this increased exponentially during World War II. Still, no one in my family ever spoke of experiencing any hostility or stigma because of their ethnic origins. Both my grandfathers had fought in the Civil War; I believe our family members felt that they were one hundred percent American, regardless of their German surnames.

I'm guessing that my relatives, like most immigrants, had come to this country to start a new life, had done so, and found no reason to look back, or make any claims about their heritage. We pre-Baby Boomers, grew up as rootless, generic "Americans." In my family the only sense that we had any real history was preserved in the food my grandmother cooked: strudels, kugels of all kinds, potato water coffee cake, heavy gravies and meat sauces. Yet, no one made anything at all of this.

Chain of Rocks Canal And Lock 27

The next day, Saturday, August 18, we started out fairly early, eager for the momentous event of going through Lock 27 on the Mississippi river. By now the four of us were in synch in terms of setting up and breaking down camp. Luckily, Harold and Bill were both easy going, both good campers, and though both were partial, as we were, to rising more toward the crack of noon, rather than the crack of dawn, they were always ready to helpfully pitch in or make the extra effort when it was needed.

As we neared the confluence of the Missouri and Mississippi, we found ourselves paddling past cliffs and rocky bluffs. Beautiful homes with sumptuous grounds lined the shore on both sides. Some had broad walkways leading down to white cottages on the river. Boats and launches bobbed gently by long docks or were suspended near some of the houses. Around nine o'clock we came to the confluence where the green waters of the Mississippi grew cloudy then dark with the silt of the Big Muddy. It seemed to me then and it seems to me now that the

Mississippi was the smaller river and was really a tributary of the Mississouri, albeit a big one, and not the other way around. There are many geographers who agree.

We stopped to take pictures, ate some lunch, studied the charts, and then headed off into the wind for the entrance to "The Canal." This, the famed Chain of Rocks canal and Lock 27 at Granite City, the last, most southerly lock on the Mississippi before New Orleans, is a thousand feet long and about a hundred wide. The water in the canal is maintained at an artificial level by twin locks. The river in the old days had run over a series of bedrock shelves here and in the summer it often had been too shallow for larger traffic like the steamboats and, later, towboats and barges. It could not be dredged so a canal with a lock was built off the northeastern shore to insure safe passage around the shallow stretch.

The four of us were subdued paddling these last few miles to the canal. The skyline of St. Louis had come into view. There was no arch, of course. We went under the Chain of Rocks Bridge with its huge cement piers, and now we saw just ahead to our port side a huge concrete chute, which was the beginning of the canal. The water in the canal was maintained at an artificial level by twin locks. The river in the old days had run over a series of bedrock shelves here and in the summer it often had been too shallow for larger traffic like the steamboats and, later, towboats and barges. It could not be dredged so a canal with a lock was built off the northeastern shore to insure safe passage around the shallow stretch.

We came to the lock. I was excited. For me, for all of us, this was a first. Jerry said it would just be like an elevator ride, a water elevator.

What about the fragility of our canoes among the huge towboats and barges using Lock 27 to the tune of hundreds a week? There were signs posted about keeping safe distances and the procedures for raising the lock gates and flooding the lock area. Still, it was good to see several small motorboats ahead of us whose pilots seemed comfortable with the fact that huge barges were looming over them. All we had to do was paddle into a clear spot and wait for the water to rise in the first compartment, then paddle the short distance to its twin and wait for the water to drain and deposit us back level with the river ahead, fifteen feet lower than we had been.

There were barges, towboats, and pleasure boats of various kinds all around us now. A warning sounded and low pitched engine noises filled the air. There were men standing on the decks of the barges and boats, hands on hips in an attitude of patient waiting. After a moment we began to rock gently as the water level rose. It was like being in a giant bathtub, filling from a hidden source.

"Hey! Where you bound for?" yelled a man from a nearby Criss-Craft.

"New Orleans!" we chorused.

He and his friend had come down river from St. Cloud, Minnesota.

"Would you like a beer?" he asked.

We definitely would. It was a hot day and the beer was cold and not only tasted great, but introduced a sense of camaraderie among us. Time passed quickly as we all talked back and forth and before I knew it we had crossed to the down-river section of the lock, been lowered to river level, and were paddling out onto the Mighty Mississippi!

IV

SAINT LOUIS DOWN TO NEW ORLEANS

I had thought the Missouri was muddy—it was nothing compared to the turbid water we were paddling through now. I half expected to draw my paddle out at the end of a long stroke and see the blade eaten away. An oily, fetid smell came to us on the wind and to my left I saw a wide stream of grayish water flowing downstream; it was laden with condoms and untreated sewage. I called attention to it and we all laughed: welcome to the big city! But it wasn't funny.

The city of Saint Louis rose up all around us. As I searched for a place we could dock, I saw rafts of barges were moored along the riverbanks in almost a solid line and realized I hadn't really given the barges their due respect. I could see we would have to go in close to them to dock and this was when I took a good look at the wide, undershot, or raked, front ends. The current was strong and any small boat, like the *Queen*, for instance, that somehow became pinned against the raked front, stood a chance of being sucked under.

A short time later, near mile marker 180 just beyond the McKinley Street Bridge, I saw a marina named the Mound City Boat Yard. As we paddled I made sure we gave the barges moored just downstream a wide berth. Jerry talked to Captain Cook, who owned the marina. He cut quite a figure with his white suit, gold braided cap, shock of white hair, and full gray brush of mustache.

"I'm afraid I can't help you boys. Your canoes might get damaged by other boats pulling in."

Jerry, not to be put off, told him a little about our trip. He shook his head somewhat dismissively. He had been a yacht captain and a chartered guide for a number of years in various parts of the world, he said expansively. Wealthy sportsmen and celebrities still called on him whenever a voyage was into difficult waters. The dangers he had encountered were truly amazing, so he led us to believe, all the while dropping names of celebrities and exotic destinations.

He paused eyeing us. Satisfied that we were suitably impressed, he said gruffly, "Well, I suppose, maybe . . . if you can follow my rules, maybe you could sleep in the shop."

"What about the dock, eh, privileges?" Jerry asked.

Captain Cook shrugged. Jerry offered him a beer, which we didn't have. Not to be outdone, the good Captain offered us all a drink—a splash of Knob Creek in paper cups. He broke out some wooden chairs and we all sat on the dock, talking about being, "on the water." The Captain inveighed against the state of boating and the world in general; Jerry did a bit of subtle inveigling. He agreed with Cook in everything he said for a time. Then he saw to it that the conversation veered from deep sea fishing restrictions to hunting regulations in the West. Cook began expounding as though he were the expert. Jerry brought him up short on a point he had belabored and that put him on the defensive. After playing him awhile, Jerry showed some fellow feeling on the topic. He now had Cook seeking his approval. By the time we left the dock to go up into the river front area to find a place to eat, the Captain had said that we could stay three days at no charge.

I relate this business of Jerry and Captain Cook locking horns because it was so typical of my friend's persuasive powers. Harold and Bill hadn't seen the Deacon operate before, but I knew exactly what he was up to. Both of us understood how important it was that we have some place to dock the boat for a few days without worrying about it.

Having secured our boats and our sleeping quarters, we did what we could to make ourselves presentable and went up the dock gangplank to explore the city. I phoned my Uncle, Roy Mueller, to tell him where we were. When I had called several days back, telling him of our trip, he had insisted we all come for a visit. Now he said he would be driving down from Marissa, Illinois, a town some sixty miles across the river to the east and south, to pick us up early in the morning.

I was excited at the prospect, but also a little nervous about how it would all go down.

Meanwhile, this was Saturday afternoon. We took in the sights, ate a long lingering meal, and walked out onto the streets after dusk. As the night came on the riverside area grew lively.

Family

Amazingly, the next day we managed to finish our breakfast and get to the designated rendezvous spot by eight o'clock. Uncle Roy's black Cadillac pulled up and we all piled in. I made the introductions and my uncle formally shook hands all around. He had a lot of questions about our journey and the ride to Marissa went quickly.

Marissa is the small town where my mother grew up. Her mother, my grandmother, Julia Sauerwein, had died a few years before this, but most members of the family still lived there. Uncle Roy was mayor of an even smaller town a few miles away named Fayetteville. He also owned its only gas station and garage, which he ran by himself as the town's sole mechanic. Another hat he wore was that of District Game Warden. He and my aunt, Gussie, had a "club house" on a fairly good-sized lake, which was really a dammed off meander of the Kaskaskia River. Jerry noted in his journal that Roy was formal, but with, ". . . a perpetual smile on his face, relaxed, not tight—owns 300 acres near town, a wildlife preserve, takes pictures and knows his birds and trees. He is a bird hunter with 30 or so beagles kept in a big kennel."

My mother was the only one of the family's seven children to move out of state when she married, all the way to Colorado. The family was close knit and like most families in those days, assumed that all the children would settle down nearby when they grew up. The fact that her youngest daughter had gone to live way out West was hard on my grandmother—and on my mother as well. As a result, when my brother and sister and I were kids, she took us "home" every summer, back east to Marissa.

We stayed at my uncle Ernest's place and his wife, my Aunt Louise, prepared a wonderful roast beef dinner for all of us and several of my other relatives as well. Uncle Ernest was a big, barrel bellied man, who had worked most of his life in the coal mines. He was black bearded and fierce looking but had a great laugh. I'll never forget the sound of it ringing out across the table as we all sat there, partaking of that fabulous meal.

There were tall cold glasses of iced tea, moist to the touch, two kinds of salad, a cold potato-mustard concoction and one with crisp lettuce and firm meaty tomatoes, along with slices of cucumber and small dill pickles. There were vinegary green beans with bits of chopped bacon; there were yellow-white ears of sweet-corn, steaming as the butter melted between the kernels, golden biscuits that looked too good to eat and tasted even better, pickled beets, celery, and cooked carrots tasting of brown sugar—all this from the garden behind the house. And, of course, there was the traditional heap of mashed potatoes and the rich gravied, delicious beef.

For dessert we had homemade ice cream. But it wasn't quite ready yet. Since dusk was just setting in, people drifted out to the grassy back-yard. Two huge, cold watermelons were cut into pieces. The inner cores looked just the right color of red, juicy and sweetly solid. More of my relatives arrived: some cousins, David Lee, Larry Ray, Carolyn Sue, Betty Lou and her husband, Charlie, and their children, Debbie and Randy. Seeing them, I regretted that my brother and sister weren't there with us. Two of my uncles, Elmer and Ray stood on the back porch, listening to the St. Louis Cardinals ballgame on a transistor radio. Mr. Nagel, who employed these two uncles and my Aunt Leona as well at his market, sat near them on the porch listening to my Aunt Norma, Ray's wife, hold forth. Jerry and Bill and Harold were talking to uncle Roy. There was much eating of watermelon, talking, kibitzing about the ball game, wrestling on the lawn, hollering and joking and delighted laughter echoing out into the long-shadowed dusk.

I remember my Aunt Gussie, Roy's wife, asking me about getting married. Gussie was sharp witted and could be sharp tongued. She was kind, yet acerbic; as a boy I was wary of her rough humor. Now she said she had a serious question for me. Was I *really* getting married? How could I just give up this life of adventuring and tie the knot so young?

She persisted, weren't there a lot more rivers to go down, exotic places to visit?

I laughed, but I felt a serious edge to her teasing. Whatever I replied, all I can remember is that someone called out that the dessert was ready, and I made my escape.

Homemade ice cream.

I can tell of packing the ice in the galvanized canister of the mixer and the salt and the endless cranking by hand and the anticipation of the restless children—but the taste, the magical taste of cream, milk, eggs, sugar, fruit; the exotic, rich texture as you put that first spoonful in your mouth, the melting sweetness? Who could set that down in words?

This was my family; these were my people. I had never quite realized how important family was to my life; how much I loved them all.

The next day Jerry and Bill went swimming at the community center just outside town, which had a large pond complete with diving board. At some point we four got together to be interviewed by a reporter from the *Globe Democrat* and had our photo taken. That evening Roy and Gussie took us all out to the Club House on the lake and put us up for the night. There was a lot of hubbub. I was seeing everything anew through the eyes of my friends. Jerry was particularly impressed with the specially mounted Wood Ducks my uncle had on display. I had never really seen them before through the eyes of a hunter.

At last we were all in our makeshift beds, pallets on the floor of the Club House living room or out on the large screened-in porch. Memories of all those summers in Marissa kept chasing through my mind; I tried to fall asleep by listening to the lap of the lake water just down the embankment off the front porch. I recalled the night we were here when I was ten years old and my mother couldn't get my infant sister, Linda, to stop crying. There was talk of appendicitis and bowel obstruction and for a while it seemed we might have to drive back to a hospital. By the time Linda stopped wailing and subsided into fitful sleep, I had had a vision of her dying—and a realization of my own mortality. I, too, would die, like my grandfather had, like everyone else would. There was no escape. In a panic I got out of bed and in the dark threaded my way down the steep stairway to the dock on the lake.

Sitting there, staring at the black silhouette of the far trees, then at the starry sky, and back to the lake, I fought to still my hammering heart. It was the sound of the water lapping the shore that calmed me, the sigh of the leaves as the wind swayed the branches of the dark trees. It was nature that reassured me all was as it should be.

Back on the Water, Back in Trouble

Uncle Roy dropped us off near the marina the following day. It was early, sometime before noon, but too late, really, to make a start on our first real paddle on the Father of Rivers. And besides, it looked like rain was setting in. It seemed, therefore, that another day and night on the town in the big city was in order. If Captain Cook would let us stay on.

We found the Captain sitting behind his desk in his dim little office on the dock. He glanced up, muttered a greeting as we came in, and then looked down at his papers. This wasn't a good sign. Jerry motioned us back from the door; he was the one who had made the original connection with the Captain and he was the one to handle negotiating for a day's extension now.

We waited just outside and I could see Jerry making his pitch. The Captain was scowling back at him, but I couldn't make out what was being said. When Jerry came out, he was shaking his head. He kept quiet until we were going up the gangway.

"We've been granted a reprieve," he said. "One more night. But he wasn't happy about our stay here Saturday. Someone set off his burglar alarm."

Saturday night we had all gone out to celebrate, but Bill and I had come back early, sometime after midnight. We were the culprits. We hadn't heard the alarm. But the Captain had. And he had had to get dressed, investigate, and call it in as a false alarm.

"He told me to tell my buddies to *stay put* in the workshop," he added, grinning. "But maybe I can sneak you guys out after dark."

So it was just a matter of locating the alarms and being a little more careful.

We spent the afternoon shopping for our supplies, a week's worth, and loading the canoes. Then, under threatening skies, we walked up to the Merchant's Café for a meal. Afterward, we did what sightseeing we could, went to a place called Molly's, and ended up at the Singapore bar. It was a Monday and the Singapore was almost empty aside from a few lone drinkers at the bar and several couples in booths. I tried to ignore how dreary it was, not the exotic, interesting sort of place its name had suggested when I first saw it. We drank beer and played shuffleboard. I sat staring out the windows, watching it begin to rain.

None of us were in a particularly good mood. I think I was not the only one feeling the loss of family. The rain started pounding down, wind driven and accompanied by rolls of thunder and lightning. We reluctantly agreed that it would be a good idea if one of us went back to the canoes and secured our supplies. This kind of rain might be too much for the supposedly waterproof packs they were in. On the other hand those packs had survived more than one storm. Who would volunteer to make the mad dash back down the street and under the viaduct to the marina? Each of us sat waiting on the other. Looking into the faces of my river buddies, I could see that each had his reasons for staying. Bill, blond and intense, was brooding over his beer and close to looking around for a fight. Jerry got up to talk to several people at the bar. Harold, big and bearish, drank his beer, poised to step between his partner and trouble. At last, I pushed out of my chair and left, motivated, no doubt, more by impatience and dourness than anything else.

To the Rescue

Aside from a few gusts, the swirling wind had subsided, but a warm rain fell steadily. The first thing I noticed as I hurried through the wet night to the darkened marina was that the catwalk down to the dock was twisted and wrenched sideways by at least half a foot.

Then I saw that the canoes were gone.

I made my way down the skewed metal steps onto the dock and ran to where they had been moored. My mind was filled with scenarios of what could have gone wrong. I had seen Jerry throw a turn and two half hitches into the painters. If they had snapped, there would be strands of rope still tied to the iron mooring cleat. The cleat was bare.

I yelled through the rain for Captain Cook, thinking to ask if he had moved the canoes, but there was no answer. The boat yard office and shop were dark; no one was around. As I stood there in the rain, imagining what it was going to be like telling Bill and Harold, let alone Jerry, that we had lost the canoes, I looked downstream again carefully.

The muddy stretch of riverbank from the edge of the boat yard to where the nearest barge was tethered, a distance of a hundred and fifty yards, revealed no shape that I could possibly construe to be a canoe. Then, a little farther on, in the darkness beneath the overhang of a huge barge prow, I caught a glint of light. It had to be the *Queen*!

I jerked off my shoes and my pants, keeping my underwear and T-shirt on. The prospect of a late night swim in the dark, rain swept Mississippi would have been frightening to me at any other time. But now I was thinking one thing: I had to get the boats back before a gust of wind shifted them around the end of the barge and out into the main current. Easing into water, I tried to keep what I had seen in sight. All I could see now was a silvery shadow bobbing in the darkness against the barge's undercut prow. As I swam closer, I could distinguish another shadow beside it: the other canoe! The current was pushing both of them sideways in under the prow. Swimming up to the *Queen*, I fumbled around her bow until I found the bowline, pulled it tight to me, then reached around, treading water, to grab the other canoe's painter. With both lines in hand, I lunged upstream, swimming with one arm and scissoring my legs. Slowly, awkwardly, I pulled away from under the prow and swam with them up the river toward the dock. It took awhile, but I made it, hoisted myself out of the water and snugged the lines to the mooring cleat without any trouble. Going after the canoes might have been foolhardy, but even now doing it seems my only option.

When Jerry and Bill and Harold showed up not so long afterward, I told them what had happened and it sobered them considerably. Just whose fault it was outweighed any notion of my heroics and instantly we all began griping at each other. Then just as quickly the mood turned jovial and we were all laughing. We had cheated the river of its spoils.

Figure 4.1
Gangway to dock. Jerry packing gear in background.

The next morning, without much ado, we ate a small breakfast and began paddling out into the Mississippi. It was an overcast and muggy day, dripping with humidity. Captain Cook appeared just as we neared the end of the dock. He was smiling and seemed glad to see us.

"Did you guys have any trouble from last night's storm?" he asked.

Jerry explained what had happened. The Captain shook his head solemnly.

"You can never take this old river for granted," he said. "That's a mistake many have made and been sorry for."

Did I see a little smirk beneath his bushy mustache?

"I don't suppose you know anything about how our boats came to drift off?" I asked.

"Oh, no," he said. "I was across the river with some of my friends from the old days, a gathering of the worthies."

He was grinning now.

We paused, holding steady by the dock, while he shored up his alibi, bragging about his friends. His smugness was galling, but there was nothing we could do, really, except push off without a word and head down river.

The Upper Mississippi: St. Louis to Cairo

The next leg of the journey was, in many ways, the most difficult—for me, at least. The Mississippi stretched away on all sides. Out on this broad backed river, seen from any vantage point, even our own, we were just two more bits of flotsam and jetsam. And yet the river was not as overwhelming as I had thought it would be when, crossing one of the bridges over it, I had seen it out a car window a few years before. The banks down from St. Louis were either scrub brush and trees or steep undercuts and rocky embankments. The sandbars and dikes along the shore and in the river were numerous. I eyed the sandspits and islands. That's where we would be camping, away from the mosquitoes, up high enough to avoid the wash of the towboats and their barges. The barges passing us now were larger than they had been on the Missouri. My best guesstimate was that a "tow" might be up to 40 barges, each about 200 feet long and almost a third that wide. The tow was rectangular, generally six to eight barges long and five to six barges wide. I figured a tow, including the towboat, might be at least 1200 feet long. Of course, river traffic posed no threat to us as long as we were alert. Several times we saw huge rafts of barges, one heading up river and one down, moving toward each other on fairly narrow bends. They were obviously in communication. One yielded to the other, which ever was going slower I assumed, and they passed with plenty of room to spare. Sometimes, as we had on the Missouri, we frolicked a bit, riding the waves they left in their wake. Generally, though, we gave all barges a wide berth.

Twenty-five miles beyond St. Louis we stopped at a place called Kemmswick for a short break, picking up some extra water. After looking over the small town, we paddled on another ten miles and made our first Mississippi river camp on a sandy bank along a wooded shore. I had noticed ducks, egrets, and teal as we went along and here under the trees you could almost imagine that we had stepped back in time a hundred years.

Jerry, after our meal and as evening came on, began telling hunting stories and Bill and Harold joined in. There was talk of deer and moose calls and to my surprise, Bill stepped away from the firelight of our camp, held up his hand for quiet, and, facing out into the dark undergrowth, put both hands to his mouth. A low cry pierced the air. I had heard that plaintive shriek before, coming from a rabbit caught on a barbwire fence. Bill was using his predator call, a stubby piece of metal and wood that I had seen before in his pack but never heard. There was silence, then the cry, then silence. After a time, he nodded his head and turned slightly. We all looked in that direction. In the tall grass at the edge of the circle of light thrown by the campfire, I saw two glinting eyes and a pointed nose. Then I heard a low throated growl. He had called a grey fox—almost right into our camp.

The next morning, we made ready to set off without eating. I was slow packing up and loading the canoe. The idea, which I wasn't exactly enthusiastic about, was that we would make it to St. Genevieve, seventeen miles farther on, for a late breakfast. The previous evening had been fun and St. Genevieve promised to be an interesting place to visit, but I had no energy. New Orleans was a long way off. I had just left my family behind without really getting a chance to visit with them. Jerry noted in his journal for this day, Wednesday, August 22, that he was ". . . half sick, headache." The general mood was "grouchy and snappy." Evidently all of us were feeling a little homesick.

But there was something more to it for me. I was beginning to feel left out of the conversations that Jerry and Bill and Harold shared. Jerry and I had gone to school together and been English majors and loved literature. Our conversations had always jumped around through a gallery of allusions that included Hemingway, Leadbelly, Mose Allison, Brother Dave Gardner, Camus, and Jonathan Winters. But talk about literature and philosophy and jazz interested Harold and Bill very little. Their talk was of hunting, guns, motorcycles, racecars, in fact, vehicles of all sorts, and various mechanical gimmicks, not to mention Western geology and history, which were second nature to them. Jerry knew these subjects well; he and Harold and Bill enjoyed discussing them, feeding off each other's knowledge and expertise. Though I liked both men and our comradery was strong, I found that in the end I didn't share many interests with them. I had no real insight into this dynamic at the time. I just knew that try as I might to ignore my feeling of being on the outside, often I felt excluded.

We arrived in St. Genevieve before nine and headed straight for a café. The town was small, maybe 4000 people, but it turned out to be one of our more memorable stops. Having had our meal, we picked up our mail, loaded on water, and walked back to a little museum that we had passed by. On display were the usual collections: guns, relics, and historical dioramas. There were also paintings of the area done by an early resident. Jerry and I got into a discussion about them with a man, Mr. M.E. Zigler, who turned out to be the owner of another museum close by. He was tall and a little stooped, graying, probably in his fifties, and not shy about talking up his work. There had been an artists' colony in St. Genevieve during the 1930s, Thomas Hart Benton, whom I had to admit I had never heard of, was a famous resident, and, evidently, Mr. Zigler had been there too. These days, however, he had put aside his watercolors and oils to work in another medium: light.

"Yes, light," he repeated with a little smile. "I employ a new technique. It's called, color forma."

I had no idea what he was talking about, but I liked his enthusiasm. He led all of us over to his "museum" a few doors down the street and soon we found ourselves in a large gallery, with the lights dimmed, staring at a wall-size screen onto which Mr. Zigler projected various colors from several projectors simultaneously. He was creating abstract paintings with light. I was impressed. I had heard of light shows, but this was something different. The lights created pure colors and could be either stable or constantly shifting and transmuting from one shade into another.

After leaving Mr. Zigler, we stopped at a tavern. Time passed and at some point as we all sat at the bar, I heard someone yell out, "Jerry Sanders?"

Down at the other end of the room stood the barkeep, holding up the phone. "Is there a Jerry Sanders here?" he called out again.

Jerry, with a very stunned look on his face answered, "Who wants to know?"

The barkeep turned to repeat the question into the phone, then said, "It's your mother."

That got a laugh.

But the barkeep wasn't joking. Jerry's mother was worried about him because a letter to Jerry's uncle, Hugh Adams had been returned. Whether it was her letter or one Jerry had sent was unclear, but either way she was worried something had gone wrong and had decided she needed to talk to him. How many places she called before hitting the jackpot, I don't know (actually there weren't that many taverns in town), but she knew we were due in St. Genevieve and she knew we would be likely to drop by a bar—to beat the August heat. And lady luck had done the rest.

Jerry, as he came back to join us, shook his head in disbelief and chagrin. But I knew that, though he would never let us see it, not in a million years, he was touched by her concern. His relationship with Lois wasn't always smooth, but he cared about her deeply.

We left for the river shortly after that. I think we all shared the thought that there is nothing like a call from Mom to put the quietus on a big night in town.

Up early the next morning, we gathered ourselves in earnest to make a hard push. We stopped for water at Chester. A man filled our jugs for us from his hose. When we told him we were on the river, he gave us a stern warning. "You get on down past the end of the Mississippi and the water gets *real* rough!" We thanked him for the tip and went on our way, making it fifty more miles to a little place called Apple Creek where we camped. All of us were in a much better frame of mind by now and felt we were focused on our journey again and back at full strength.

It helped that we now hit a few days of cooler weather. The heat and humidity had taken a toll on us, even though we were out on the river most of the time where a breeze, if there were one, could find us. We made Cape Girardeau easily the next morning. We shopped and stayed there for lunch. I bought a new paddle and Jerry lingered a long while in Summers Gun Store.

Clouds were gathering, however, as we headed back for the river and paddled into the current. The day grew steadily darker as the sky filled with black billowing thunderheads. The rain came in a sudden downpour. Heading into shore, we sheltered for a time in a boxcar on a railroad siding, then decided it had let up enough to continue down the river. An hour later another storm began to move in. When I saw a barn not too far from the riverbank, I headed us for it. Tying up the boats, we walked to the nearby farmhouse. It was Jerry, as usual, who stepped up to the door. His knock was answered by a broadchested, bearded man, who gave us all a stern once over. Clearly, he was not used to strangers of any kind appearing at his door, let alone seedy looking characters in ponchos like us. I could see two teenage girls, his daughters I assumed, peering out at us from the stairs behind him. His place was some distance from any town and he had a right to be wary. Nonetheless, he invited us in out of the rain.

We all stood just inside the door in a kind of vestibule before the stairs while he questioned us and listened as Jerry described our river trip. The man's name, as we were to soon find out, was Paul Homarth. Paul's rendition of being a gruff patriarch was pretty good. Still, as Jerry told our story with the two daughters, the oldest of whom we overheard was named Judy, looking on from halfway up the stairs, he gradually gave in to his basically hospitable nature. We could sleep in the barn that night. But there was one rule we had to follow without fail. There would be no smoking, not even pipes. The hay in the barn was tinder dry and rain or no rain, the place would go up in a flash. We assured him: absolutely no smoking. Satisfied, he threw on a rain slicker, led us outside, and shoved back the broad barn door. Inside it was dimly lit, but spacious. He showed us a stack of neatly folded horse blankets, then said, "Remember: no smoking," and went back to the house.

The barn, used mainly to store hay, had that aromatic alfalfa smell. Mr. Homarth had turned on the light, a single naked bulb suspended from a rafter, instructing us as he did so not to leave it on. I could see as I gazed around that there was nothing fancy about our sleeping quarters, hung with tackle, pieces of equipment, and various tools. But, considering the rain pelting down now outside, the place seemed luxurious. Each of us chose a soft spot for himself, and, after a trip to the canoes for gear, set about spreading out our damp sleeping bags. We had some fruit to share, and bread, but that was it.

Late afternoon had set in, the day was dark and there was very little to do but sit by the door, watching the rain fall—or trying to catch a glimpse of one of the daughters at the lighted upstairs windows.

"Wasn't she a beauty?" Bill said. And I knew he was talking about Judy.

"I wonder what she might be thinking about us," Harold said. "Four guys off the river crouched out in her barn, staring at her bedroom window."

We all laughed.

"Yeah," Jerry said, "you guys don't have any girls waiting for you when you get back home, go ahead and fantasize."

Not that he wasn't as smitten by the lovely farmer's daughters as the rest of us. But he was thinking about Betty. And I thought about Gloria. If only she could see me now.

But things were different for Jerry and Betty than for Gloria and me or so I thought. She and I had plans, definite plans. Jerry and Betty were not sure what the future held for them as a couple or separately. I know he loved her and that she loved him, but at twenty-three neither of them was ready to settle down. Betty wanted to get her masters. Jerry? I had never met anyone more adventurous or more determined to see the world than he was. He went on, in fact, to travel the world in one of the most adventurous styles possible. But that's another story.

Jerry, when he did marry was going to be one of the most faithful and diligent of husbands. I knew that would be true, and he knew it, and he knew he had better get the fascination of far shores and exotic peoples out of his system before he married. So he was torn in his relationship with Betty. He loved her but his love fought with his longing to take chances and reach out and engage the wide world. He devoured Betty's letters, reread them, and burned when no letter came, yet he felt it was beneath contempt to complain of feeling neglected and even told himself, or at least me, that it didn't matter.

Our conversation about Judy was interrupted by the thud of a distant door closing. It was the front door of the house. A moment later Mr. Homarth stepped into the barn.

He carried a large wooden tray before him and on it were four coffees, bowls of chili, and big slices of German chocolate cake. He set the tray down on an upended barrel and we thanked him profusely, if awkwardly. It seemed like a meal fit for kings. After eating, I climbed into the loft and lay a blanket on the alfalfa. Rain fell steadily on the shingle roof, hard at times, driven by wind gusts that made the old barn shiver. I fell asleep content and grateful, knowing it could have been another truly terrible night in the tent.

The Homarths were simple, straightforward folks, and I will never forget their kindness. Later in my life I had more than enough opportunities to learn just how callous and cruel people can be. On such occasions, I've tried to remember people like the Homarths, who showed me, early on, the other, redemptive side of human nature.

The next morning we woke early, seven o'clock. It was a day of good news and bad news. The good news was that a breakfast of delicious coffee and pancakes awaited us. The bad news was that we had to empty four inches of water out of the canoes. Everything was soaked. And it began raining as we shoved off.

We made it down the river to Commerce, Missouri, another small town, and looked up a laundromat to dry out our clothes and bedding. We took up positions in Jean's Tavern until around two, by which time the sun was out and the world looked like a much more promising place. Taking off again, it was only a few hours before we began looking for a campsite and found one on a sandbar. All our gear needed to be spread in the sunlight and we were busy until dusk reorganizing it.

The next day, August 26, we paddled to Cairo, Illinois. It was an important marker on our journey. First of all, for navigational purposes the Corp of Engineers has divided the Mississippi River into two halves, the Upper Mississippi and the Lower Mississippi. The Mississippi River's mouth where it flows into the Gulf of Mexico some 95 miles south of

New Orleans is called, "Head of Passes." From this point, distances on the Lower Mississippi River are measured in statute miles "above Head of Passes." On Jerry's navigational charts, this was abbreviated as "AHP." Cairo, Illinois, is at mile maker 954 AHP, and Cairo is considered the dividing line of the lower and upper sections of river. We had paddled from St. Louis, which was at mile marker 184, and had now gone past mile zero, which was the end of the Upper Mississippi, to mile 954, beginning of Lower Mississippi.

Secondly, the river that we were on at this point had changed, literally as well as navigationally. The Ohio River ends its 981 mile journey from Pittsburg here at Cairo; where it converges with the Mississippi, green water meets brown water. The Ohio is the wider of the two rivers at Cairo and comes close to doubling the size of the Mississippi. It is here and from this point forward that Old Man River really takes on his legendary size.

The Lower Mississippi: Cairo to New Orleans

If New Orleans was 95 miles above Head of Passes, then of the 3,800 mile journey we had begun, there remained 859 miles of the Big River to paddle. That's a long ways, but we were now beginning to get a sense that we actually might make it. We redoubled our determination to start out early, during the morning cool, when the temperatures were still below eighty. Then we would paddle four or five hours, pulling over to rest or go into a town until after the sauna-like heat abated later in the afternoon. We were caught between wanting the trip to be over and wanting to slow down and savor the journey, now that the end of it was almost in view. We spent more time swimming, exploring the riverbanks, and many an afternoon we lounged about in small towns, just looking around and talking to people. The following selection, describing the three days near Cairo, is fairly typical of what we were experiencing during this time.

Jerry's Journal, August 25-29

Left Commerce about 2:00 and paddled in semi-jovial mood till 4:00; hung up things to dry. Found bottle with a note in it from girl in Elmo, MO, confiding love in God. Slept in wet blanket and was damn miserable. Up early. Hot and humid, pushing into Cairo, 33 miles. We drifted for the last three. Cairo fronts on the Ohio River and we camped on a sandbar on a chute that formed an island off the Mississippi. Camp was just across from a towboat. All four of us paddled in one canoe across the chute to the boat—a real ball! The towboat guard took us to town in a truck. We washed & dried our clothes, got mail and the man was good enough to give us a ride back to our boats. We all sat on the tug and talked until sundown. Bill got out his predator call when we got back to camp. The towboat man, when he heard some kind of critter or varmint out in the dark answering, ran his light around trying to spot it.

Monday, August 27. Paddled on to Wickliffe, Kentucky for supplies and breakfast. A woman named Rose Smith interviewed us during breakfast. These journalists seem to pop up from nowhere. The druggist at RX store gave me cards and paper free. We left at 10:00 and hit the blue cold water of the Ohio. Pulled along side a friendly commercial fisherman and guide, talking about this and that, he demonstrated his goose call, a pretty effective holler. Gave us fish for bait, cut and dyed red. We camped on an island, five miles below Hickman, Kentucky.

Tuesday, August 28. Harold was up before dawn to go hunting, shot one dove. We traded bow paddlers on this day. Friendly towboat captain gave us a little fresh water. Harold and I hit New Madrid at 12:15, way ahead of Bill and Rich. They were still back on the New Madrid Bend—a twenty-four mile loop. Finally they caught up and we all went into town, ate and looked around. Took in a movie, first all summer: *The Man Who Shot Liberty Valance*. We got more water and went on; made 38 miles and camped directly across the neck of the loop—one mile—from where we started. I was told earlier it would be channeled soon.

Wednesday, August 29. Paddled to Caruthersville by 3:00. Still have Missouri on west side of river; they call this the bootheel country. We went to town for supplies and water, which we got from a toothless fisherman. His wife was younger and had kittens all around the house. We walked to a place called Doc's for a beer. Some idiot drunk kept "teasing" the barmaid. Camped six miles below Caruthersville. Our little radio says lookout for rain. Joke at the end of news about report of U.S. being in South Vietnam, telling of corruption of Diem Gov.: "Man, what kind of action is that over there— those cats aren't fightin' soldiers, they're fightin' Go-rillas."

Thursday. Planned a big push. Awakened at 2:00 a.m. by thunderstorm, vicious rain. Crawled under the overturned canoe on beach. Slept on wet blanket until dawn. Miserable.

It rained hard, intermittent, until 2:00. We pulled out at 3:00. Total miles: about seven. Sat and read and talked. Harold went hunting, shot an egret, skinny, no down, small. Went on to Heloise Ferry crossing at Heloise, Arkansas. Ate a sandwich at E.R. Moody's general store. As we talked, he told us that when he was a boy he had gone to Oklahoma with his parents in a covered wagon—and back. "Yasser, a fur piece."

Pitched our tents, but too hot and humid inside. I slept out.

It seemed we could not get past the state of Missouri. We had first encountered it below Rulo, Nebraska on the lower Missouri river. For a time we paddled between Nebraska and Missouri, then it and Kansas. From Kansas we paddled all the way across Missouri, almost 500 miles, to St. Louis, so we had Missouri on both banks of the river for ten days or so. Later, after entering the Mississippi at St. Louis, we were between Missouri and Illinois, then it and Kentucky, then, finally, it and Tennessee. When we did actually get past the so-called bootheel of Missouri, I felt all traces of the Midwest slip behind us. We were moving deep into the South now and not only was the countryside changing, becoming more lush and jungle-like, the people we met were now distinctly,

"Southerners," part of a culture I was familiar with from my father's side of the family. He was born in Western Kentucky. My brother, Steve, had been born there, and during World War II we had lived in Norfolk, Virginia, where my father worked in the Portsmouth shipyards as a welder. I was six when we moved back out West.

It turned out Jerry's roots were in the South as well, at least partially, since his mother, Lois Adams, was from Arkansas, where she still had family. She wanted Jerry to be sure and contact her brother, Hugh, when we reached Memphis and this was our next destination.

Heading past the bootheel country, paddling with Arkansas on one side and Tennessee on the other, we agreed that no matter how spirit-damping the continual rain storms might be, we would make Memphis by the second of September, two days from now. We would roll out before 6:00, make breakfast, man the canoes, and shove on past Blytheville, toward Osceola. As we approached the latter, we came on an Arkansas fisherman who hailed us. Or at least he hailed Jerry and me. Bill and Harold were miles behind us as usual.

"Wanted to tell you something," he yelled. And when we got closer he said: "They's a red k-new come past here 'bout two hour ago, two boys in it from off the Ohio. You part of that bunch?"

We told him we had come down the Missouri and into the Mississippi at St. Louis, but thanked him for the information. Did he know anything about Ashport, the next town down?

We were looking for clean water since what we had taken on at Heloise had proved to be full of rust. He said that Ashport was small.

"You daren't blink when you get there cause if'n you do, you'll miss it."

We went on, and two hours later we had the red canoe insight. Pulling along side, we introduced ourselves and found out we were talking to Keith and Jim from Youngstown, Ohio. They had put in at Pittsburg, pretty much on a whim. They had come part of the way hitching rides on towboats and even at times on yachts. They had no tent, they said, and had been through, as we had, some terrible weather. No tent? And I thought we were the ultimate of minimalist shelter with our pup tent.

As I took a closer look at them and their gear, I saw they actually looked to be in pretty bad condition, though they made a show of enthusiasm as they described their adventures.

We talked awhile, then took photos of each other and paddled on. Soon they disappeared behind us, back around a bend. Strangely, Bill and Harold did not come across them. We wondered if they had pulled in somewhere.

Ashport was, indeed, a small place and pretty much isolated. We pulled into a sand beach and by the time Harold and Bill arrived the rain had set in again. We all sheltered in a bar called the Gold Dust. There were several local men there and, of course, they wanted to know what we were all about. Someone asked if Jerry and I had seen any real "Injuns," being from the West and all. Instead of answering directly Jerry said he had read that Osceola, the town we had passed by just up the river, was named after an Indian. A man who was a warrior and statesman and had figured importantly in the Seminole wars down in Florida. No one at the bar, including me, had any idea what he was talking out.

"We do have a few breeds around about," said the little man behind the bar. "Red, yellow, brown, mostly no-account."

The other men nodded. This was the first time the subject of racism had come at us, front and center, though we were to encounter it often as we went on. Jerry paid the barkeep's comment no attention. He grinned and said he had read that Osceola had been tricked into coming into a fort for a peace parlay and then put in prison where he died. The men were unsure whether he approved of this as a clever stratagem or thought it was downright evil. The bartender, alert to keeping the peace as all good barkeeps are, intervened at this point with some question about where we had set out from today. I think Jerry, judging by what he told us later, was probably the only one of us who realized how close we were to real trouble.

As I said, I thought I knew the South and Southerners pretty well and that the Civil War was over and something to read about in a history book. My years in college had taught me liberal, or what I would call to this day sane perspectives on issues of race. I had read about the Freedom Riders, I had written a paper in college on Governor Orval

Faubus. I had been incredulous, as were most of the people I knew, upon hearing about his attempts to block school integration in Little Rock. Sending out the National Guard to keep children out of school? Ridiculous, as Charles Mingus put it in, "Fables of Faubus."

I was aware, too, that James Meredith, because of the color of his skin, had been stopped from entering the University of Mississippi, a state owned school. He was waging a legal battle to gain entry and that battle was raging as we sat talking to these men. Undoubtedly, I thought I held the high ground on the question of equal rights for all under the law. But I was not going to try making converts of these Gold Dust boys. They weren't sure where we stood, since we were from the West. We let it stay that way. They goaded us, but we laughed them off.

I, for one, slept poorly that night. I lay in the tent for hours, listening to rain fall on dark, roiling water. A light came sweeping around the far bend, flicking shadows along the brushy embankments. The light seemed to be searching, hunting for me, but I knew it wasn't. I knew that up the dark river a towboat pilot sat in his cabin chair, intent on his course, looking for channel marker buoys, throttling back his engines so as not to swing wide and drive his long tow of barges onto a sandbar. The throb of his engines came nearer and nearer. Then it passed and faded. There was only the sound of the rain and the river and occasionally the watery hiss of what I knew to be a whirlpool, rising, spinning fast, and then vanishing.

Hardly had I fallen asleep and it was time to get up. We were hitting the river early, determined to make a push into Memphis. As it turned out, paddling as hard and consistently as we could, we didn't quite make it. We paddled 56 miles and camped within six miles of our goal.

The next day we docked at a marina just off Joe Curtis Point near downtown Memphis and Jerry went to find a phone. His Uncle Hugh lived about an hour away over in Arkansas in a town named Brooklyn.[17] When Jerry called, Hugh insisted he would be driving down to pick us all up. He had strict instructions from his sister, Lois, to take good care of us. That was fine with me. This was Sunday, September 2. After

---

17   As fate would have it, I was to see Brooklyn again some nine years later when I lived near it in Jonesboro and taught at Arkansas State University.

almost three months on the river with only three nights off, a little home cooking, a bath, and a dry bed sounded good.

We made arrangements at the marina for securing our canoes and Jerry called friends of his family in Memphis who picked us up. The next day we piled into his uncle Hugh's '55 pickup and crossed the bridge from Tennessee to Arkansas, the bridge we would soon be paddling under, and drove into West Memphis and on between the low land cotton fields toward the little town of Brooklyn. The crops looked scruffy. The shanties beside the road did not look livable, and yet there were children playing around them. This was where Howlin' Wolfe and B.B. King grew up. Blues country for sure.

It was crowded at the Adam's house, but we were welcomed heartily and encouraged continually to make ourselves at home. The Adams clan was almost as large as that of my own family back in Marissa and now, trying to keep names and faces together, I got to see what it must have been like for Jerry when we were there.

I remember a superb chicken dinner, a luxurious hot bath, and a wonderfully comfortable bed, but overall this day went by in a haze of unfamiliarity. By the time we were back on the river Tuesday, I was not feeling well. Bill, Harold and I had diarrhea—too much high living all at once, evidently—and Jerry and I were irritable with each other. To season the situation to perfection, it started to rain just as we got on the water.

We made twenty-two miles despite all of that and pulled into a sandbar and flung up our tents. It continued raining all night.

The next day we started out paddling hard and by noon we were past Tennessee and had Mississippi on our left hand shore. The river was amazingly wide here and slow, even in the chutes or cut-offs. It demanded a steady effort of bent back and long reach paddle strokes if we were to make any distance.

After lunch on the water, the wind came up, blowing down river. Tired as we were, we decided to try the sail awhile. Harold and Bill had outfitted their canoe with a sail, too, and they joined us, hoisting up Bill's yellow slicker. We started out together, a flotilla of two, but soon they fell miles behind us. Sailing, even with a good wind, generally proved cumbersome for them. They enjoyed it when the wind was right, but otherwise the sail required constant adjustments.

We did fifty-one miles. Arkansas was still on our right hand shore and Jerry and I reached Helena at 6:00, far ahead of Bill and Harold. There was nothing to do but wait idly. Gazing along the shore, I saw a mile marker and did the numbers quickly in my head—only 591 miles to New Orleans. We could do that in ten days, or definitely in two weeks without fail. And this thought was followed immediately by one that I tried to push aside: the thought that I wanted this trip to be over—now. I found I had developed a certain litany about the towns along this section of the Mississippi, just as I had with the dams on the upper Missouri. *Only four more big towns to go, Greenville, Vicksburg, Natchez, and Baton Rouge.* I went over the names in my mind dozens of times, focusing on the number four.

Four more towns. We were almost there.

Meanwhile, here we sat waiting. A half an hour passed and Bill and Harold hove into sight. Having to wait for them every day in order to have lunch on the river together or make camp—this too was beginning to irritate me.

In this mood I helped set up our tents near the boat dock. We strolled into Helena and sat down to a six-bit meal at Nick's—and a very good meal at that. Feeling better, I went out with the others to look over the town. Jerry and Bill and Harold went into a store whose owner was proclaimed on the door to be Mr. Robert E. Lee, Gunsmith and Locksmith extraordinaire. I followed them in and listened as Mr. Lee told us of his own river adventures, sailing and racing canoes. He had made a voyage from Cairo to Baton Rouge and spoke of the dangers. "Quicksand," he said. "Quicksand, boys, is what you got to watch for when you camp on sandbars."

I had thought of quicksand as something movie heroes fell into as villains pursued them through the jungle—in other words, a semi-mythic man-eating sand pit. This wasn't the case, according to Mr. Lee, and what he said was confirmed by others we spoke with on down the river. The fact was that as the river rose, the current ate away at the base of a sandbar, or sand island, and slowly the lowest layers were permeated with water, changing the consistency of the sand to slush. This watery sand-slush could be ten or twenty feet deep. As you stepped out onto it, the sandbar surface appeared solid. That surface, however, was only a crust and once you put your weight on it you plunged into—yes, quicksand. There was no way to get any purchase on anything, nothing to grab but crumbing sand and the more you struggled to climb out or "swim," the faster you were sucked down and drowned. He had once seen a deer right along the bank get caught and go down and disappear.

"You're lucky though," he said with a wink. "This is September and the river level is going down, not up. So you boys should be okay. But y'all have to always test a bar to make sure."

He was launching into his stories about snakes along the river when I faded toward the door. Harold walked out with me and we decided to trek back to camp. The Green Apple Quick-Step was still visiting both of us and it had been a long day.

Jerry's Journal, September 5

Helena, Arkansas—quite a town. Met Robert E Lee, full of tales about the river and why folk fear it. Stopped next door at the bar for a short one. Harold and Rich went home at 9:30. A drunk phoned the local paper editor name Jack something and he showed up in a straw carnie type boater with little straw balls dangling from brim. His first comment: "I hate that river!"

We all laughed and the stories commenced to roll out of him non-stop. This man could talk—and drink (many a Wild Tom he put down). Told of how Texas was annexed by Crockett and Houston, all about Crowley's Ridge near town here, five hundred foot above the delta floor and site of glorious Confederate victory at Chalk Bluff. The stories kept coming, very funny man. Spoke of the *Sprague*, at Vicksburg, greatest of all the riverboats. We had to go up the Yazoo canal, he said, when we got to Vicksburg—site of the most important battle of the Civil War and place where Confederates used first electrically detonated underwater mine to sink the

Union ironclad, the *USS Cairo*. Claimed there were at least two dozen Civil War ships beneath the waters of the Yazoo River. I ate at Nick's again and made it back to camp at 1:30. Cold, 60 degrees.

That next morning, a Thursday, gray clouds and the rumbling threat of rain greeted us as we got up, cooked our *Mom's Coco Wheats,* and hit the water by 8:20. This was a long day. Jerry had little to say, aside from telling me about the newspaper editor with the funny hat who thought he was Mark Twain. I knew he was getting impatient with the journey, just as I was. For a long while in the afternoon we waited for Bill and Harold to show up, talking about our friends back home, and pointedly avoiding, as we usually did of late, any mention of our girlfriends. It began raining and we kept on reminiscing. Finally, the silver canoe with our two intrepid partners in it, flailing away at the river, came into view. I figured they must have been at least twenty miles behind us.

We set up camp in the rain, something we were used to doing by now, though long habit didn't make it any more pleasant. Then we took some gear back into the trees where it was drier and made our supper, mac and cheese, baked potato. Unfortunately, if we ventured any distance away from the river, we were a feast for the mosquitoes, no matter how much repellant we put on.

Friday began a little differently. For one thing we had hot sauce eggs for breakfast. For another we had come upon a section where the current was a little faster and we challenged Bill and Harold to a competition for the day. We would paddle their canoe and they would take ours.

Now there would be no excuses about "canoe design."

Right away I noticed a certain heaviness to their boat as we cut through the water. It was unwieldy. Try as we might to paddle with a bit more vigor and reach the level of ease that we had in paddling the *Queen*, we quickly fell behind. After just a half day of pushing hard, I had to admit that their excuses were valid. Their canoe was a turkey. As they had said, it was hard to paddle because of its extra width. Jerry and I did manage to keep them in sight most of the time. Still, they hove in to make camp around 4:30 and were waiting for us with big grins and a horselaugh or two.

Interestingly, we almost lost the canoes that night. The river rose at least a foot while we slept beneath the mosquito bars. Luckily, we were up earlier than usual, 6:30, and snagged them before the mooring stake could wash out completely. I was left wondering though: did this rise in the river mean we had to watch out for quicksand?

That day, Saturday September 6, began with our little radio predicting rain and strong wind gusts. We were only thirty miles from Greenville and figured we would make town before the worst of the storm hit. We made ten miles in almost three hours of paddling, had an early lunch, and paddled on.

Just before the rain hit, the wind began blowing hard. We were moving through a series of sandbars and the wind whipped the sand at us. Thinking it would quit, we paddled on. But the wind increased. Bizarrely, we were in a major sandstorm with visibility at near zero out in the middle of the Mississippi River. This kept up until it started to rain, wetting down the sand. And for the first time on the trip, I was actually grateful to have the rain roll in.

Before long we pulled into the little harbor at Greenville, Mississippi called Lake Ferguson, which is really a silted off meander of the river. We set up camp on the embankment and started off for the road to town, only to realize that we had a treacherous stretch of marshland to cross. Finally, we came upon a road and were lucky enough to catch a ride. Or, as Jerry put it in his journal, ". . . hitchhiked in with two yahoos in a '54 Plymouth."

Picking up our mail, water, and a few supplies, we went down to the Greenville dock area along the lake and it wasn't long before one of the marina operators offered to give us a ride back to camp—on the water. His name was James McCloud. James told us to pile into his boat, a red Glasspar speedboat with a 75 horsepower Johnson motor on it. It was a strange feeling to be kicking up so much wave and wind action, roaring along ten times faster than we could have paddled. The boat's top speed, according to Mr. McCloud, was almost 70 miles an hour. We all looked across at each other.

"At this speed," Bill yelled, "we could be in New Orleans in a little over . . . seven hours!"

We laughed, but none of us were about to suggest selling the canoes and getting a real boat, one with a motor. As I thought about it later, I saw that we not only appeared to be, but were, an anachronism. We were proud of the fact that we were paddling every single inch of the river from Three Forks to New Orleans—but why? Wasn't it in a way a boyish and romantic idea, mostly bravado? We certainly met people along the way who thought so. I never argued the point, nor did Jerry or Bill or Harold that I knew of. In some unarticulated way we knew there were rules, self-imposed perhaps, that had to be followed if you wanted to have an authentic encounter with the river.

The call to adventure might include a call home for money or a night or two in a warm dry bed, but it did not include an outboard motor doing the work for you, not if you hoped to gain the respect of those who had run the river before you. There were rules; you could fudge them, but just a little.

Surely, the voyage really wouldn't have meant as much if we didn't do it the old-fashioned, Huck Finn way. More than once I repeated that to myself.

Back at camp, we put up our mosquito bars, hoping to sleep outside under the stars. But there were no stars to be seen. Just after midnight it began to rain. Into the tents we went; then, when the rain stopped and the sky cleared a little, we took to the mosquito bars. Many nights were like this as we kept trying to beat the heat and humidity and sleep out in the open where we could get the occasional cool breeze.

The next morning, Sunday, we had *Malt-o-Meal* for breakfast, just to break the monotony.

We shoved off beneath a low, gray sky draped with darkening clouds. The wind came up and we were hit by squalls. For a while we drifted. The rain was warm and with the wind whipping around, it felt good, cooling. We swam and cavorted a little. When the rain ended, we took to shore to make a meal. Just as we finished the wind came up again, hard, gusting. My hat and the grill we had been using became air borne, ending up somewhere in the river, never to be seen again.

The grill? Well, luckily, Bill and Harold had brought one much like ours so now we would use it. But my hat? My fine wide brimmed straw hat Gloria had mailed to me when Jerry and I were just entering Nebraska? I was glum about losing it. It had come this far down the river only to be stolen by the devilish wind that had been sniping at us all along the way.

Getting back on the river, we managed to make 43 miles. We passed beyond the Arkansas state line, and though Mississippi was still on the left, and would be all the way to the Gulf, we now had Louisiana on our right. These were the last two state borders we would travel before New Orleans. Realizing this we decided to redouble our efforts tomorrow and make Vicksburg.

Monday, September 10, we were up at daybreak and soon on the water. It was hot and humid, but we paddled on, the gray, cloudy sky threatening rain at any moment. By two o'clock we had done 32 miles. We waited for Harold and Bill to catch up, had our lunch, swam a little, and by 2:00 we were hard at it again, nearing Vicksburg with the two of them nowhere in sight. Jerry, however, as a precaution, had made sure to tell our companions that we wanted to end up at the Yazoo river docks and had marked the canal that would lead them to it on their map.

Around 6:30 industrial buildings on the horizon above the trees told us we were there; then a waterway appeared on our left. We figured this was the Yazoo Canal and paddled up it. About the time I was sure we had taken a wrong route, a dock area came into view. Soon Jerry had made arrangements for securing the canoe and even wrangled the four of us a place to sleep. Still, Bill and Harold were nowhere to be seen. If they had missed the turn off, or somehow passed us they would end up God knows where. As we waited, we talked it over. How would we track them down?

A half hour later they came paddling into view, grinning, coasting serenely into a berth beside the *Queen*. That night we all slept on the *Sprague*.

Figure 4.2 The Sprague, September 1962

It is surprising to me at my present distance in time, that we actually were allowed to spread our sleeping bags on the deck of this historic vessel, the *Sprague*, the greatest of the steam driven sternwheeler towboats in the world. It had set a world's record for pushing 60 barges of coal in a raft that covered 6 acres and was a 1000 feet long. It was decommission from service in 1948, and when we slept on its deck in 1962, it had been permanently docked riverside in Vicksburg as a museum and exhibit center. Sadly, it was partially destroyed by fire in 1974. People concerned for its beauty and historical value mounted efforts to restore it but these failed. In 1980 the Corps of Engineers dynamited the *Sprague* and removed its remains from the river.

I have a vivid memory of this boat, its pilot's cabin and the massive wheel at its stern that must have been a wonder to behold as the boat powered upstream, pushing its tow. The four of us went on the official tour of the boat the next morning, then went through a museum close by and toured an antebellum home. The history of the South was on display in many places. The Rexall drugstore where we bought a few items even had a collection of rare weapons in the rear. A more troubling part of Southern history was on display at the Riverside Café.

It was a little Greek place, a diner. We had seen it the day before and now we decided to stop in for lunch. It seemed like our kind of inexpensive greasy spoon. Approaching it, I noticed there were two doors to the place, but made nothing of it. We stepped through the right hand door, and I came to a sudden halt; we all did. Before me at the counter sat only black diners who turned and stared. I stared back. Then one of the black men motioned across to the other door. We had entered the "Colored" section of the café.

Surprised and confused I stepped back outside and the four of us went around to enter the "Whites Only" door. Inside, we were met by several questioning, even hostile stares from men sitting at the counter who were able to see clearly where we had tried to come in. Suddenly, the racial issues in the South, and all over our country, were staring me straight in the face. Not quite knowing what to do, we took seats at the counter and ordered. Right across from us in the center of room, was a green plywood partition that reached down from the ceiling three or four feet, bisecting the café. The cooks worked in the back and a server moved down an aisle between the two sections, waiting on first one side, then the other. The principle of separate but equal could not have been put into practice more graphically. There was no discrimination, in that diners on both sides were fed and served equally. The only problem was that I ate my food looking across at men and women on the other side of a barrier that announced they were different and didn't have the status I had as a human being. It would be a year before President John F. Kennedy called for a federal civil rights act and two years before President Lyndon B. Johnson, on the heels of Kennedy's assassination, was able to get the bill enacted into law. As we walked out the door of the Riverside Café on that September day in 1962, Jim Crow was alive and well.

All four of us were shocked and left feeling threatened. The dehumanizing and pernicious nature of what we had just witnessed couldn't have been made any clearer. I went over the scene in my mind the rest of the day, but in the end it seemed there was nothing to do about it except remember it, and use that memory to speak out or act when I could for racial justice.

So I was a tourist in the land of racism. Explorers and adventurers were, I realized, basically tourists, curious to observe the beauties of a foreign landscape and the strange ways of the natives. Essentially, it was not a tourist's place, unless cornered, to take responsibility for anything happening around him or her.

I felt uneasy about staying over another night in Vicksburg, but I agreed to it. The next day, Tuesday, we spent sightseeing. Evidently, I left the others in the evening, as Jerry wrote in his journal, "to go to a show." I don't remember going to a show, or movie, at all—though I may have. What I do remember is walking through a black neighborhood after dark. There were lights in the houses on both sides of the narrow street and voices singing out now and then in loud and lively dialogue, but the streetlights were very dim and far apart.

How I came to be in that area or where I was going has fled my memory, but I do remember a song that was playing so loud I could hear it all along the street. It was "Green Onions," by Booker T and the MGs. I walked along through the dark, listening to this song, which still has the power to get me out of my seat and moving my feet, wondering about the lives of the people in the houses I passed.

I felt a low-key excitement and I felt afraid. What would happen if I encountered someone, if someone yelled at me from one of the dark porches? I had grown up in an area called Poverty Gulch, what today would be called a Barrio part of town. Still, I was a young white, liberal college kid who saw himself as an opponent of racism. None of that cut any mustard here. I was just a crazy whitey in the wrong part of town.

I kept walking. No one bothered me and I ended up, at some point, back at the *Sprague.* That was my most singular encounter with racism on our voyage, and it was mainly, as I was to understand years later going over my fears of that night, an encounter with my own inner racist.

The next day, Wednesday, we shoved off from the dock early. We ate on the river, breakfasting on sandwiches we had bought in town. In the middle of this meal, Bill and Harold came close to being run over by a tow heading downstream and were treated to a string of epithets, ending with: "You idiots!"

More than once, Jerry and I had worried about them because their canoe was unwieldy. For their part, they just laughed. As they saw it, the river here was over a mile wide. In order to hit them, that tugboat pilot would have to aim right at them. *Come on.*

This day, as usual whenever we left a town, we made poor mileage, pulling over early to camp on a large sandbar. I remember it distinctly because when I crawled out of the tent that morning I saw in the sand a wide, sinuous trail leading past the tent peg and down to the water. It looked like someone had dragged a heavy stick in S curves the width of the sandbar down to the river. A snake had passed by on its way to drink. Or had the snake come *out* of the water and passed by the tent, hesitated, as it sensed a warm blooded presence inside, and feeling mellow gone on its way?

Spooked, I handled the gear carefully as I went about loading the canoe. It was a relief to get back on the river again.

That day, Thursday, we came into Natchez. We walked in for water and noticed that here, more than any other place, people on the streets gaped at us. Clerks came out of stores we passed to take a good look. Had the Martians landed? Wasn't it a little early for Halloween? We had no camera and could only scowl or grin in reply. When we got back to the canoes, Jerry did get some good photos of the river, which looked to be several miles across at this point.

The heat out on the water was intense. So much so that the gunwales were too hot to touch. Around four o'clock we decided to pull into a sandbar. It was early and hours before we could think of camping so we made a decision to run on the river at night. This wasn't a good idea because we had no navigational lights. Still, there would be a cool breeze on the water after the sun went down. We were sure we could avoid the occasional tows pushing up or down the river, and, judging from what we had seen during the day, there would be very little debris large enough to be dangerous. Bill interrupted the discussion at this point to assure us he'd be ready with his rifle if we ran up on an alligator. That eventuality hadn't occurred to me.

Jerry shot at bats as dusk came on. The moon rose slowly and as it did we shoved off.

Paddling at night in the moonlight on the black-silver surface of the Mississippi, we lost all sense of the horizon. We were just slipping on and on into darkness with only the sounds of the water flowing and the ripple of the paddle rising and falling, going faster and faster it seemed into the dark coolness of night without effort: this was one of my most memorable experiences of the trip. It was great to be alive, fully alive, and I felt all we had endured was worth it.

Jerry must have felt the same way, I heard him begin singing an old tune, maybe a Leadbelly song like "Goodnight Irene," or was it the one called, "Careless Love?" He knew dozens of songs, had a good voice and loved to sing, but this was the first time I had heard him do so for a long, long time.

We paddled in tandem with Harold and Bill for the last hour, then pulled in to shore about 2:30. It turned out we picked a poor spot to camp. The lights, yellow and white, in the distance which we had thought signaled a towboat rounding the wide bend, actually belonged to a revetment crew working a third shift. By the time we realized this, it was literally too late to get back on the river again so we finished putting up the tents and tried to sleep despite the distant glare and the constant noise.

Up early, having slept hardly at all, we made a quick breakfast and shoved off. As we passed the revetment crew, several of the men waved, then we were on down the river, one deliberate stroke after another. I was drenched in sweat, groggy, and every movement of my paddle was an effort. Soon, from behind me, farther out in the river, I heard a ker-plunking splash and turned to see Harold in the water. On the instant I laid my paddle along the gunwale and rolled off into the river. The water was not very cold, but it was at least wet and cooler than the torpid air. After a time, Jerry and Bill joined us and we let the canoes drift as we swam in slow circles around them. Swimming was cooler than paddling but more tiring. By three o'clock, back in the boats, we pulled into shore on a wide sandbar to make camp.

We had just set up the tents and had something to eat, when I glanced over the water and spotted the white wake of several powerboats coming up river. I was surprised when the boats suddenly changed course and headed right toward us. Veering into shore, they cut their engines and the lead boat idled into the sandbar right in front of us.

We stood there, the four of us in shorts, and watched five uniformed men bail out of the lead boat and move purposefully into our camp. The men all carried rifles and made no effort to hide them. The leader, a man wearing a cartridge belt, a Stetson, and a black vest with an official looking badge on it, stepped up to us, carrying his rifle casually in the crook of his arm.

"Have you boys seen anybody along here," he said. "Maybe in a row-boat?"

We said we hadn't. Several of the other men, rifles at the ready, were cautiously approaching our tents, bending to look inside. I noticed now that there were two dogs in one of the boats, beside a man who was obviously their handler. They had to be bloodhounds.

The leader watched us steadily and said nothing more. When the other men, rifling our tents pretty thoroughly, were satisfied they held nothing more dangerous than sleeping gear, they backed slowly toward the boats, keeping their eyes on the undergrowth along the shoreline.

The man in the Stetson continued to stare at us.

"Y'all better be keepin' an eye out," he said. "We've got a man we're after. He stole a boat and he might just be along close by, you hear?"

Stole a boat from where? He didn't say and we didn't ask.

"Well, Sir," Jerry said. "We haven't seen a soul."

The man eyed him for a moment and said, "Alright. But don't be camping on this side of the river." He turned and pointed down river behind him. "You gona be safer tonight on over t'other side."

The other men were climbing back in the boat, but their leader stood waiting for Jerry to answer. Jerry nodded, assuring him we understood and would shift ourselves pronto. The man turned away then and climbed back into his boat.

He grinned at us as he sank down behind the steering wheel.

"Okay, boys. Ya'll have a nice day!"

And with a roar of outboards he and his party tore off upstream.

Before they were out of sight, we were packing up and setting out for the West shore. We found a sandbank pretty much like the one we had just left and pulled up to it and got out of the canoes. What, exactly, had just happened? We started to talk it over. I was feeling the incident was like something out of a movie. It would be five years before Paul Newman would make *Cool Hand Luke,* but we had just seen the previews.

As we talked it out, we decided we were not in any danger. After all, the man on the run was going upstream of us and he wasn't going to be landing on this side of the river surely. But if he did, where would he be going? Was there actually any place near us that he could be heading for?

Jerry grabbed his maps out of the *Queen.* We stood around him as he pointed to tiny letters at the base of the long, thumb-shaped bend we were on.

"That's Louisiana State Prison," he said. "It can't be more than two or three miles away."

None of us knew that it was called Attica, the Alcatraz of the South, that it was the largest state prison in the country, that it had once been a slave plantation covering 60,000 acres. None of us had ever heard of it. And all we really cared about at the moment was checking to make sure there were no towns close along this side of the river. Seeing that there were none, we felt better. Still, it seemed like a good idea to put some distance between the river posse and us.

As we pushed on in our canoes, dark clouds were massing to the west behind us. We knew we had to find a campsite soon, but this wasn't easy. The riverbank was generally a tangle of dense foliage. Sandbars and islands were becoming harder to find. So when we saw a Corps boat ahead, we decided to see if we could wrangle some shelter under the pretext of asking for water. The men on the boat turned out to be friendly and talkative. We had their attention right off with our tale of the river search. They hadn't seen the posse or heard anything over their radio about any escaped convict.

They were from Greenville. Not only did they fill our water jugs, but they also roused the cook and he made us a meal of meat and potatoes. Looking out the pilothouse windows as we sat talking and eating, I saw the storm closing in, with wind swept rain pelting hard toward us. What a pleasure it was to sit there in the little pilot house at a table, warm, dry, eating, then listening to music and talking about songs while the storm raged outside. By around ten that night, a calm had set in so we got back into our canoes and shoved off.

If the Corps boys thought it was not such a smart thing to do, running the dark river with no lights, they didn't mention it to us.

About ten miles farther on we spotted a wide, moonlit sandy beach at the head of a looping bend and a safe distance out of the ship channel. As late as it was, we just put up the mosquito bars and slept in our clothes, ponchos for a ground cloth and sleeping bags for mattresses.

The next morning, just after sunup, we set out for Baton Rouge. Actually, there was no sun to be seen. The silvery gray sky began to darken as soon as we were on the water, and when we were about four miles from town, we ran into bad rain and worse wind. All we could do was pull over to shore and hunker down among the trees. As with many of the storms we encountered, there was a dramatic lightning display with this one. I wasn't fond of lightning. Not then and not now. It is unpredictable. It lurks up inside those dark clouds like an angry sizzling fist, preparing to sucker punch you at any moment.

As the four of us talked about its power and stories of people who had been zapped multiple times, I realized, either through someone's comment, or just by putting two and two together, that water is a good conductor of electricity—and so is aluminum. All the way down the river and down the lakes, I had thought a lightning bolt striking the canoe would just disperse harmlessly, like it does when it strikes a car, where it circles the vehicle's metal frame and via the so-called Faraday effect, goes to ground. As an occupant you're safe—unless you are touching metal.

Wouldn't the same thing happen in a boat?

"No, not bloody likely, Mate," Bill said, trying for an Aussie accent. He explained that since you would be bound to touch some surface on the canoe, the lightning coursing through it on its way to ground itself in the water, would juice the boat's metal, melting some of the fixtures, and, no doubt, frying its occupants.

Though I argued with him at the time, I later learned he was right. If lightning wants your boat, it may hesitate a millisecond over whether to hit you, who are not so good a conductor, or the aluminum of the boat, which it loves. But in either case you will end up toast. Being out in an aluminum boat on a wide, open lake or river where you are obviously the highest thing around is pretty much like sitting on top a lightning rod.

My come back to Bill was. "Oh, yeah? Then why don't fish get struck by lightning?" Harold just looked at me and shrugged. Jerry, by way of commenting on my anxiety, climbed a low limbed tree near by. What a pal. It was only years later with the advent of the all-knowing Mr. Wizard, *Google*, that I actually found a definitive answer to my question. I happened on a report of Koi found dead in a pond. This led me to the 1941 article in *Copeia* called, "Mortality at Fish Hatchery Caused by Lightning."[18]

Yes, fish do get struck by lightning—quite often.

Even without knowing this gruesome fact, I felt grateful as I hunkered there under the trees by the Mississippi River, that I had not been smart enough to worry about lightning until that moment.

Spared by the storm, we went back to the canoes and found almost two inches of water in them. We bailed it out and headed on, stopping at Red's Boat Store. All along the banks of the river now were refineries and chemical plants. Actually, you couldn't see the banks because they were crowded with barges, sometimes four and five abreast, and for the first time—ships.

We had been told we would see them in Baton Rouge, which was 230 miles from the Gulf and as far up the Mississippi as they could go. At Baton Rouge these freighters, many of them international in ori-

---

18 "Mortality at Fish Hatchery Caused by Lightning", Edward C. Raney, Copeia, Vol. 1941, No. 4 (Nov. 21, 1941), p. 271.

gin, were busy unloading and reloading. Many were at long platforms, where cranes swung pallets or steel containers on board, while others were linked together and anchored in the river. These ocean going vessels from all over the world are around six hundred feet in length, not as long as some tows, but they are three to four stories tall. That is what impresses you as a canoeist paddling along beside them: looking, up and up and feeling like a tadpole next to a whale.

There were no marinas in this area and finally we ended up sleeping on a docked towboat. We were running into more and more people, interesting people that I couldn't help seeing through the lens of various novels I had read about the South, particularly William Faulkner's.

A short quotation from Jerry's journal, may serve to give you the flavor of our time in Baton Rouge.

> "Bill couldn't cash his check. We met Ed Price, had his glasses taped at the bridge and tied on with string. Told us to try Western Union, which worked. Warned us to watch out for lepers below Plaquemine. Drank in a bar that had three guitar players and met a woman who said she married her husband because he fell in her lap. Her sister, tough, yet, innocent looking, left in a big Cadillac with the bar's one-legged owner. It was a long, wild night."

The next morning, groggy and tired, we pulled out about 10:30. The sea-going ships were definitely intimidating. Looming up on both shores, they were sleek metal behemoths. Overwhelmed by their shadows, we paddled stealthily past. I was imagining how we must look from high up onboard one of these ships, when two things happened almost simultaneously.

First, we saw the red canoe of the paddlers from Ohio. It was up on the bank, bottom up. We never learned whether they had ended their trip at Baton Rouge or gone on.

Second, someone began yelling. A tugboat had pulled up behind us and the crewman was shouting at us.

"Stay away from those ships!"

And: "They will run over you!"

The tug kept its distance beside us and the man, friendly but terse, gave us the lowdown.

"They are three times faster than tows and they run silent. You can't hear them coming, especially if they're behind you. Understand?"

We understood and thanked him. The tug moved off slowly, passing us yard by yard as we made a manic pretense of trying to keep pace with it.

Paddling on down the river, I noticed it was narrowing, and therefore, getting deeper. The dikes, which generally we had not seen because they were out of sight back in the underbrush and trees, were now in full view on both sides. This had to do with the Corps' chief engineering task below Baton Rouge, which was to keep the channel deep enough for the international freighters.

I kept wondering, could such enormous ships really be that quiet?

After thirty miles of paddling in the high heat and hundred percent humidity, we pulled into a point that was nothing but hard gumbo mud, got out, and began rummaging through the grub boxes for something to eat. The plan was to stay off the river and rest in the shade until the moon came up around nine o'clock, then do some night paddling.

The time passed slowly in the heat. I couldn't help thinking of Gloria and our upcoming wedding. I hadn't seen her for four months. I had changed and I found myself opening the box where I kept her letters, searching through them for any sense that she had changed. Wasn't it a little crazy to get off the river and get married right away?

I was sweating and pestered by insects. All of us were tired; there was no hope of grabbing a nap. Dusk came on, then night, a very dark night, since the moon had not yet risen. Just as we were preparing to get on the water, Harold brought our attention to something. "Look," he said, "What is that?"

It was a white blur emerging far down the river, slipping around a bend with no sound, no engine noise at all: a ship.

I watched it coming on, growing larger by the second, and heading directly for us, phantom-like, ghost quiet.

We stood staring at it.

"You know," Jerry said, "I think we are in the shipping channel."

We were. Moving quickly we stowed the few things we'd carried ashore and shoved off. Even at that, the massive towering prow of the ship was on us before we had gained more than two canoe lengths.

A moment later it slid powerfully past and its wake came rushing our way. Jerry and I dug in, pivoting the *Queen* to meet the undulating waves bearing down on us, trying to take them at a right angle. I saw Harold and Bill following suit. The rolling waves looked to be higher than those we had encountered with some of the big towboats, over four feet high.

All of us were prying water with our paddles, working fast. For a time we rose and fell in the dark; we were getting splashed, soaked with no way to tell where we were, a very eerie feeling. The heaving waves rushed on past our two canoes and hit the gumbo shore we had just been on, inundating it, time and again. Gradually, they subsided.

Paddling on down river, lesson learned, we drifted for a while, waiting for the moon to rise. We passed the lights of a landing and a town on the Louisiana side of the river. I knew this must be Plaquemine, the town where, as Jerry noted, Ed Price had told us to be on the lookout for lepers, a very odd remark, even for Ed.

Years later, in the 80s, I heard about the establishment of the Gillis W. Long Hansen's Disease Center at the site of the former Louisiana Leprosarium at Carville, Louisiana. Hansen's disease is leprosy; Carville is just south of Plaqueville. The Carville leprosarium had been established on an abandoned sugar plantation on the eastern side of the river at the end of the nineteenth century and had, by the time we passed it, only a few remaining occupants. It was sobering to read that although leprosy was never a major disease threat in this country, two full-fledged medical centers were built to treat those who had contracted it and to give humane refuge and enlightened treatment to sufferers. Some victims of the disease and their families lived there all their lives. I wish I had known this at the time on the river. I might not have laughed along with Ed the way I did. But as I have pointed out before, it took me awhile to learn a thing, and learning to spot stigma and see through the way it dehumanizes people is an on-going study.

As we drifted, the moon, almost full, finally came up. It was only a spectral glow. Fog had rolled in along the banks and over the water so that the way ahead, even when bathed in moonlight, had become a shifting, curling, lambent gray wall. We paddled on through it for a time, but as we neared Donaldsonville Ferry, it became so dense we decided it was dangerous to continue. We had to make camp.

This wasn't easy in the dark. We ended up pulling both canoes out of the water and up the side of an embankment, beyond the range of any passing ship's wake; then we climbed to the top and set up our tents. The mosquitoes were swarming us. It was impossible to keep them out of the bars as we set them up and that made for a hard night.

On Monday, September 17, we made breakfast on the embankment top, then retrieved the canoes, which had weathered the night with no problems. We made about thirty miles, passed a bridge that was under construction and shortened our route several times by taking chutes, which saved us from going around bends. One of these, however, having filled from the other end with silt, was a dead-end. There were a good many shallow bars here and the water was so full of fish that we could see their finny backs as they swerved away from our paddles. Worse, the narrowness of the chute encouraged mosquitoes and made it hard to turn around so we had to back paddle fast.

The next day I was awakened by a rifle shot followed by a squeal. I crawled out of the mosquito netting to see Harold just at the edge of the sandbar bending over what I thought was a large muskrat. Bill said it was a nutria, or coypu. I had read about this animal in my muskrat trapping days. Fur farmers had introduced it to the states from South America, it was valued for its fur and its meat, but inevitably someone had released it into the marshes of Louisiana and it had multiplied exponentially. In 1962 it hadn't yet been deemed an invasive species with a bounty on its head. Harold thought we might skin it and cook up some of the meat, just for curiosity's sake, maybe as a kind of memento. Bill and I objected. Still, Harold was right, in that since this was going to be our last day on the river we should come up with something appropriate to the occasion.

Later, we talked it over. There was nothing to drink by way of a toast aside from some tea left from breakfast. Someone, probably, Bill or Jerry, suggested memorializing the day with a photo. We progressed from joking about holding up the dead nutria by the tail, to hoisting a victory flag and ended with the photo you see below—apologies to Joe Rosenthal. We knew we hadn't done anything even approaching the heroism of those soldiers on Mt. Suribachi, who fought to liberate Iwo Jima, but we wanted to make some kind of iconic statement of how we felt about the battles we had waged with the rivers.

Figure 4.3 Celebrating

By nine o'clock we were on the water and, according to the next mile marker I saw, eight miles from New Orleans. We paddled along expectantly, but nothing along the riverbanks changed. We were passing what looked like the same trees, dikes, and levees we had seen for the past week. Then, coming around a bend, we were suddenly there. Amazing! Just ahead I saw hundreds of barges and docks, loading platforms, ships and massive shipyards. The Huey Long Bridge loomed up and over the river. All four of us were shouting. This was it, New Orleans, Queen City of the South.

We had made it!

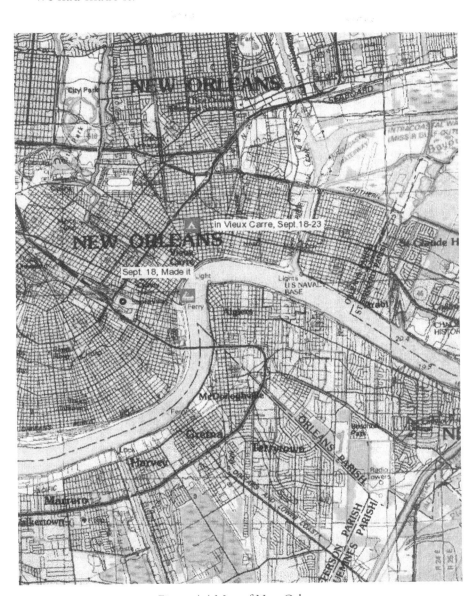

Figure 4.4 Map of New Orleans

I wanted to remember this moment all my life. A photo wasn't enough to mark it. I turned in my seat and what came to hand first was the damnably heavy Dutch oven that I had lugged around for almost four months—a 106 days to be exact. I grabbed it and flung it out as far as I could into the river. I felt a tug of sadness along with my defiant exaltation as it sank to the bottom.

New Orleans

Overwhelmed by the sheer scale of the harbor and feeling outclassed by every craft we saw, especially the great ships from many nations, we made our way with as much dignity as we could to the Corps docks and there got permission to secure our boats.

Figure 4.5 Harold Umber, Bill Shirley, and Jerry Sanders

A Mr. Webber took us along to the post office. Leaving the post office, letters in hand and a package or two, we headed off for the nearest YMCA, hoping to find a place to celebrate along the way. The first place we came to was a black people only grocery and tavern. The woman running the store was adamant about our not coming in. She gave us directions to what she called, "a colored Chinese laundry." That didn't exactly make sense, but none of us were in any mood to argue. We decided to go there, wash our clothes, and go out on the town later, in style.

Thus, ended our voyage on the big rivers and now began our adventures in New Orleans. We went to Jackson Square and the Starving Artists café, stayed a long while at Pat O'Brien's, and for three days did little more than enjoy the city. It was an adventuresome time of a different kind, and through it all I kept trying to take in what we had accomplished and make it feel real. We had actually done it; here I was in New Orleans, 3,800 miles of river behind me. The journey was over, the grand enterprise was finished. Now I had to get on with the rest of my life—and my choices would be more complicated.

Bill and Harold hitch-hiked back home, Jerry's brother "Red" arrived to drive him back, and I, the first to leave town, took the bus. It felt strange to sit there in that bus without my river partner, watching the passing countryside, seeing how the season had shifted seemingly overnight to autumn. Something inside me had changed as well. I was not the man Gloria had waved goodbye to, I had learned things about the world and about friendships, and about myself, some of which I never fully realized I was learning until this writing, things that became part of me without my knowing it.

I had also thought a few things through. Now that the river had had its way with me, I had another voyage in mind, beginning with a wedding I had to go to, if my beautiful fiancée would still have me. I hopped the bus on Sunday, the twenty third, and we were married six days later on September 29 in Glenwood Springs, Colorado. Jerry D. Sanders was my best man.

ABOUT THE AUTHOR

Richard E. Messer earned his Ph.D. at the University of Denver. He has pursued post-graduate work in Analytical Psychology at the C.G. Jung Institute in Küsnacht, near Zurich. A poet, fiction writer, and literary critic, he is a Professor Emeritus of English at Bowling Green State University. His work has appeared in many journals, including *The Nation, Psychological Perspectives, The Sun*, and *The Black Warrior Review*. He is the author of three books of poetry, *Murder in the Family*, (1995) which was awarded the Nancy Dasher award by the College English Association, *A Life on Earth*, (2006) and most recently *Dark Healing*, published by il piccolo editions in November 2013.

Also by Richard E. Messer

Dark Healing

Murder in the Family

A Life on Earth

Also by Genoa House

SPIRITUALITY/SELF-HELP

When Pixies Come Out to Play: A Play Therapy Primer
by Lois Carey, 1st Edition, Trade Paperback, 280pp, 2014
—ISBN 9781926975115

A Salty Lake of Tears: A Soul Journey
by Lois Carey 1st Edition., Trade Paperback, 112pp, 2011
—ISBN 9781926715476

PSYCHOLOGY

Solar Light, Lunar Light: Perspectives in Human Consciousness
by Howard Teich, 1st Edition, Trade Paperback, 120pp, Index, 2012
—ISBN 9781926975054

ASTROLOGY

Capricorn Rising: Productive Poet, Scientist, Mentor
by Kathleen Burt, Trade Paperback, 108pp
—ISBN 978-1926975092

Beyond the Mask: The Rising Sign Part 1 & 2 (Combined Edition)
by Kathleen Burt – Astrology/Spirituality, Trade Paperback, 394pp, 2012
—ISBN 9781926975085

PLAYS

Out of the Shadows: A Story of Toni Wolff and Emma Jung
by Elizabeth Clark-Stern, 1st Edition Trade Paperback, 70pp, 2010,
—ISBN 9780981393940

FICTION

Feasts of Phantoms, by Kehinde Ayeni, 1st Edition Paperback, 350pp, 2010
—ISBN 9780981393926

Soul Stories by Elizabeth Clark-Stern, 1st Edition Trade Paperback, 160pp, 2011
—ISBN 9781926975009

Main Street Stories, by Phyllis LaPlante, 1st Ed., Paperback, 238pp, 2010
—ISBN 9780981393919

52769986R00107

Made in the USA
San Bernardino, CA
28 August 2017